ITALIAN TWO EASY

The River Cafe

ITALIAN TWO EASY

Simple Recipes from the London River Cafe

Rose Gray and Ruth Rogers

Photographs by David Loftus
Design by Mark Porter

Clarkson Potter/Publishers
New York

Introduction 6

Mozzarella 8

Salads 16

Salted, smoked &
dried fish & meat 36

Tomato pasta 58

Fish pasta 76

Really easy soups 100

Fish with . . . 124

Birds with wine 144

Roast meat 164

Grilled fish & meat 186

Italian vegetables 204

Baked fruit 230

Lemon desserts 246

Chocolate & coffee 258

How to make . . . 276

Italian pantry 279

Suppliers 280

Index 282

Introduction

Italian Two Easy is the second volume of simple recipes from The London River Cafe. It was in Puglia, last May, that we mapped out the chapters and wrote in our notebooks the easy and delicious recipes we wanted to include in this, our sixth cookbook.

Over the year we had traveled to cities and regions of Italy, both familiar and new—to Verona for Vin Italy, the huge wine fair; to Milan, to immerse ourselves in the tradition and sophistication of a city that takes food so seriously; to the Cinque Terre on the coast of Liguria for a family wedding; and to neighboring houses in the Val d'Orcia in southern Tuscany, cooking with our friends and family.

Our first chapter, Mozzarella, like the Bruschetta chapter in *Italian Easy,* is simply a putting together of ideas using a few seasonal ingredients—all quick, easy, and delicious ways to begin a meal with mozzarella.

For us, salads are simple combinations of vegetables served at room temperature—grilled, boiled, roasted, slow-cooked, and raw. In this chapter, there are boiled potatoes with anchovies and capers; fine green beans cooked until soft, then mixed with lumps of local hard cheese; and an unusual toasted bread and arugula salad with olives and vinegar.

Recently at The River Cafe, we have increased our range of cured meats and salamis. We have also started to use traditional smoked fish such as eel and haddock, cutting them like Italian carpaccio and bringing out the flavor with olive oil and lemon juice.

In Puglia, we found tomatoes used in practically every dish, and it was there that we decided to devote a whole chapter to tomato pasta. We have included a summery spaghetti with raw tomato and arugula, a winter pappardelle with pancetta and cream, and two recipes for preserving tomatoes.

Throughout Italy, there are interesting variations combining fish with pasta. Every cook and restaurant has their own version of spaghetti vongole, and we have included the versions we love—with white asparagus from Verona, fried zucchini from Rome, and broccoli from Naples.

We always have a soup chapter in our books. In this one, many are meals in themselves, robust and distinctly regional. A chickpea soup we had eaten in Milan was a delicious way of cooking chickpeas with a piece of pork. In the same restaurant we found the pappardelle soup with borlotti beans. And in a trattoria in the market we had an intriguing soup of just red wine and broccoli—no bread, no herbs, but, as the chef told us, one crucial clove of garlic.

We have called our fish chapter Fish with . . . In Tuscany, we ate our favorite strong-flavored fish—red mullet—with olives and anchovies; in Puglia, we were surprised to eat a kind of sushi—thin slices of raw tuna with just a piece of bruschetta and lemon; and in Liguria, we loved the simplicity of boiled langoustines with just olive oil and sea salt.

We nearly always cook game birds with wine, looking for flavors in a particular wine to complement each bird. This is the first time in one of our books that we have suggested the variety of grape. Some of them are international varieties, but all are produced in Italy.

For the roast meat chapter we have returned to traditional recipes such as pork cooked in milk, using the fattier shoulder instead of loin, and vitello tonnato, this time spread with a concentrated tomato and basil sauce or a strong mayonnaise flavored with anchovy rather than tuna.

The flavor of the grill on meat and fish is very Italian, which is why we have put them together. Grilling over hot coals outside in the summer is quick and easy. It is all about simplicity—you take a fish, a bird, or a steak and either marinate it or brush it with olive oil using a rosemary stick.

From the beginning, our passion for vegetables has been at the heart of The River Cafe. The first thing we do when we arrive in Italy is find the local market, which perfectly reflects the season and the region. As every Italian cook has many recipes for the same vegetable, we too have included more than one way of cooking zucchini, porcini, potatoes, and eggplant. All are easy and rely on the quality of the vegetables.

The last three chapters of the book are devoted to desserts. Baking fruits is a way of concentrating their flavors. We use a lot of vanilla, cinnamon, ginger, and different types of sugar, a style more River Cafe than Italian.

Lemon juice, lemon zest, and lemon extract feature frequently in the breakfast cakes, granitas, and cheesecakes we enjoy eating when in Italy. The lemon, ricotta, pine nut cake comes from a *pasticceria* in San Casciano, the vodka granita from the bar of The River Cafe. The very, very easy lemon almond cake is similar to the ones served in the cafés on the autostrada.

We end the book the way we like to end a meal—with chocolate and coffee, and those rich, indulgent cakes we know everyone loves to eat: a bitter mousse cake, a hazelnut chocolate cake, and a boozy version of tiramisu.

Every now and again in *Italian Two Easy,* we have put in a more ambitious recipe. Killing a live crab may be something you have never done, and cooking a beef shank for twelve hours or a chicken for four may seem excessive, but it is in this excess as well as in the simplicity of these recipes that we find the pleasure and excitement in cooking. We hope you enjoy these easy recipes as much as we do.

Rose Gray and Ruth Rogers

All the recipes are for four except where mentioned. The cakes and tarts are for eight to ten.

1

Mozzarella

Beet, tomato, capers
Raw zucchini, prosciutto
Fava bean, olives
Bruschetta, tomato, olives
Grilled eggplant, roasted tomato
Salami, cannellini, olives
Asparagus, arugula, Parmesan
Summer herb, crème fraîche
Red and yellow peppers, capers
Grilled fennel, prosciutto
Marinated anchovy, spinach
Celery, radish, Parmesan

Beet, tomato, capers

Boil beets until tender, then peel and slice into 1/4-inch disks. Slice plum tomatoes into similar disks. Wash the salt from salted capers; drain. Mix the capers with red wine vinegar and olive oil. Combine the tomato and beets, season, then stir in the capers and juices. Place on the plate with mozzarella, and serve with torn-up basil leaves.

Raw zucchini, prosciutto

Using a Y-shaped potato peeler, shred zucchini into fine ribbons. Mix lemon juice with olive oil; season. Toss the zucchini in the dressing, adding a few arugula and mint leaves. Place on a plate, add mozzarella, and lay slices of prosciutto over.

Fava bean, olives

Boil fava beans until tender. Drain and season; add pitted small black olives. Toss arugula and mint leaves with lemon juice and olive oil; season. Tear mozzarella into pieces. Put the leaves on the plate with the mozzarella. Sprinkle the olives and fava beans over.

Bruschetta, tomato, olives

Cut tomatoes into quarters and squeeze out the seeds and juice. Mix together with basil and olive oil; season. Pit small black olives; mix with black pepper, dried hot chile, lemon juice, and olive oil. Grill a piece of sourdough bread on both sides, then lightly rub one side with garlic. Season; pour olive oil over. Place on a plate with the olives, tomatoes, and mozzarella.

Grilled eggplant, roasted tomato

Cut plum tomatoes in half lengthwise and remove the seeds. Season with salt and pepper, and drizzle with extra virgin olive oil. Roast in a 400°F. oven for 15 minutes. Slice an eggplant into ½-inch disks and grill on both sides. Toss with basil, olive oil, and lemon juice; season. Place on a plate with the tomatoes and mozzarella.

Salami, cannellini, olives

Drain and rinse a can of cannellini beans, then gently heat with lemon juice and some olive oil. Season and purée. Pit small black olives and toss in a little olive oil. Finely slice fennel salami and place on a plate with mozzarella. Put the bean purée alongside, and scatter on the olives.

Summer herb, crème fraîche

Boil chard leaves until tender, then drain, cool, and roughly chop. Dress with olive oil and lemon juice; season. Slice mozzarella into ⅝-inch slices and place in a bowl. Add crème fraîche, seasoning, and a few crushed fennel seeds. Roughly chop a little fresh basil, parsley, and mint, and lightly stir into the cheese mixture. Place on a plate with the chard and drizzle with olive oil.

13

Red and yellow peppers, capers

Wash the salt from capers and drain. Grill a red and a yellow bell pepper until the skins are blackened. Peel, remove the seeds, and then tear lengthwise into quarters. Toss with olive oil, red wine vinegar, torn basil, capers, and black pepper. Place on a plate with mozzarella.

Grilled fennel, prosciutto

Slice fennel lengthwise into ½-inch pieces and boil until just tender. Drain and dry on a cloth, then grill on both sides. Toss arugula leaves in olive oil and lemon juice with the grilled fennel, then season. Place on a plate with slices of prosciutto and mozzarella.

Marinated anchovy, spinach

Boil spinach leaves until tender; drain
and cool. Wash and fillet salted anchovies;
add pepper, then squeeze lemon juice over.
Mix lemon juice and olive oil together and
season. Toss arugula leaves and, separately,
the spinach in the dressing. Mix the greens
together and place on a plate with
mozzarella. Put the anchovies over.

Celery, radish, Parmesan

Wash radishes and some of their leaves,
then slice finely. Use a pale heart of celery.
Finely slice the stalk and keep a few of the
leaves. Shave some Parmesan. Mix lemon
juice with red wine vinegar and olive oil;
season. Toss together the radish, celery, and
celery leaves in the dressing. Place on a
plate with mozzarella. Place the Parmesan
shavings on top and drizzle with olive oil.

2

Salads

Borlotti bean, sweet potato
Potato, capers, anchovy
Potato, green bean, tomato
Radicchio, walnut, Gorgonzola
Toasted bread, olives, vinegar
Chicory, ricotta, prosciutto
Savoy cabbage, capers, parsley
Green bean, Parmesan
Green bean, mustard
Cucumber, mint, mascarpone
Crab, fennel, tomato, radicchio

Borlotti bean, sweet potato

Fresh borlotti beans	2¼ lbs
Garlic cloves	2
Plum tomato	1
Sage leaves	2 tbsp
Sweet potatoes	1 lb
Dried hot chile	1
Dried oregano	1 tbsp
Ex. v. olive oil	

Preheat the oven to 400°F.

Pod the borlotti beans. Peel the garlic. Put the beans in a saucepan, cover with water, and add the garlic, tomato, and sage. Bring to a boil. Simmer for 30 minutes, or until tender.

Peel the sweet potatoes and cut into 1¼-inch pieces. Crumble the chile. Put the sweet potato in a bowl with the chile, oregano, and 3 tbsp olive oil. Season and toss. Place a piece of foil in a baking pan and lay out the sweet potato in one layer. Bake for 20 minutes. Turn the pieces over and bake until tender and crisp on the edges.

Drain the beans and remove the sage, garlic, and tomato skin. Return the beans to the saucepan and add 3 tbsp olive oil. Season. Mix with the sweet potato and serve warm.

We use fresh borlotti beans (also known as cranberry beans) for salads in the summer, but dried beans are delicious as long as they are less than a year old. Look for borlotti di Lamon, which have a creamy texture. Simmering, rather than boiling, helps keep skins intact. Let the beans cool in their cooking liquid to keep them moist. Add salt only at the end of cooking, or the skins will toughen and crack.

Potato, capers, anchovy

Waxy potatoes	1¾ lbs
Salted capers	3 tbsp
Anchovy fillets	12
Fresh hot red chiles	2
Lemons	2
Ex. v. olive oil	
Arugula leaves	4 oz

Peel the potatoes. Rinse the capers. Split the anchovy fillets in half lengthwise. Cut the chiles in half lengthwise, scrape out and discard the seeds, and chop. Halve the lemons. Squeeze the juice of a lemon half over the anchovies.

Cook the potatoes in boiling salted water until tender. Drain, then cut each potato in half lengthwise and in half again lengthwise. Place in a bowl and add the capers and red chile while still hot. Squeeze the juice of a lemon half over the potatoes and season. Pour on 4 tbsp olive oil and toss gently.

Roughly chop the arugula, season, and toss with ½ tbsp lemon juice and 2 tbsp olive oil. Add to the potatoes and scatter the anchovies over. Serve with lemon.

Potato, green bean, tomato

Waxy potatoes	1 lb
Plum tomatoes	12
Fine green beans	9 oz
Red wine vinegar	2 tbsp
Ex. v. olive oil	6 tbsp

Peel the potatoes. Cook in boiling salted water until tender. Drain and, while still warm, cut into ½-inch slices. Peel the tomatoes (see page 66). Cut in half lengthwise and squeeze out the seeds and juices. Trim the green beans and cook in boiling salted water until tender, then drain.

Combine the vinegar and olive oil, and season.

Toss one-third of the dressing into the beans and another third into the tomatoes. Season both. Mix the remaining dressing with the potatoes and season. Toss the beans, tomatoes, and potatoes gently together, then serve.

Radicchio, walnut, Gorgonzola

Radicchio head	1
Fresh green walnuts	1 lb
Gorgonzola	10 oz
Parmesan	3½ oz
Lemon	1
Ex. v. olive oil	

Remove the tough outer leaves of the radicchio. Cut the head in half, then shred into ribbons. Crack open the walnuts and remove the nut meat from the shells. Cut the rind off the Gorgonzola, then cut into fine slices. Shave the Parmesan. Squeeze the juice from the lemon.

Mix the lemon juice with 4 tbsp olive oil and season.

Put the walnuts in a bowl and stir in half the dressing. Toss the radicchio ribbons with the remaining dressing, then add the walnuts and Gorgonzola slices. Lightly toss, then put onto individual plates and cover with the Parmesan shavings.

Serve with olive oil drizzled over.

Gorgonzola is a blue-veined cow's-milk cheese made in northern Italy—the longer the aging, the stronger the flavor. The piccante variety is a harder-textured, stronger-flavored Gorgonzola that works well in this traditional combination of walnuts and bitter radicchio. The creamy, mild dolcelatte is delicious in sauces.

Toasted bread, olives, vinegar

Ciabatta slices	4
Arugula leaves	4 oz
Small black olives	¼ cup
Fresh hot red chile	1
Garlic clove	1
Ex. v. olive oil	
Red wine vinegar	2 tbsp
Thyme leaves	1 tbsp

Preheat the oven to 425°F.

Cut the crusts off the bread. Wash and dry the arugula. Pit the olives. Split the chile in half lengthwise, remove and discard the seeds, and finely chop. Peel the garlic.

Put the bread on a baking sheet, drizzle with olive oil, and toast in the preheated oven for 5 minutes. Turn over, drizzle with a little more oil, and bake until brown, another 5 minutes. Rub the toasted slices on one side with the garlic clove.

Combine the red wine vinegar with 6 tbsp olive oil; season. Put the olives in a bowl with the chile, thyme, and 1 tbsp olive oil.

Break up the bread, and put in a bowl with the arugula. Toss with the dressing. Add the olives.

We vary the dressings for salads depending on the ingredients. With this salad of bread and olives, use red wine vinegar rather than lemon juice, as it has a sweetness and sharpness that goes well with the olives.

Salads

Chicory, ricotta, prosciutto

Chicory	**9 oz**
Young spinach leaves	**9 oz**
Lemon	**1**
Ricotta	**scant 1 cup**
Ex. v. olive oil	
Prosciutto slices	**8**

Break the leaves off the chicory. Remove the stems from the spinach, then wash and dry the leaves. Squeeze the juice from the lemon.

Mix the ricotta in a bowl with a fork to break it up. Add half the lemon juice and 3 tbsp olive oil; season.

Mix the remaining lemon juice with three times its volume of olive oil.

Put half the spinach leaves in a bowl and toss with the lemon dressing. Lightly mix the remaining spinach leaves and chicory with the ricotta sauce. Add these leaves to the other leaves and gently toss together.

Serve with slices of prosciutto draped over.

Chicory has a distinctive bitter taste. The family includes Belgian endive, radicchio, catalogna, scavola, and the wild version, dandelion. Catalogna, a less well-known variety with long, pointed green leaves, is the most bitter. Use the tender hearts and small leaves in this salad. We cook and use the larger outer leaves like spinach.

Savoy cabbage, capers, parsley

Savoy cabbage	**1 small**
Salted capers	**2 tbsp**
Flat-leaf parsley leaves	**4 tbsp**
Red wine vinegar	**2 tbsp**
Ex. v. olive oil	**½ cup**

Discard the tough outer leaves of the cabbage. Cut the cabbage in half and remove the core. Slice the cabbage very finely. Rinse the capers in a strainer under cold running water. Chop the parsley.

Make a dressing with the red wine vinegar and olive oil. Season.

Toss the cabbage with the dressing. Add the parsley and capers, and toss again.

A jar of capers in salt is one of the essentials of the Italian pantry. Use them in sauces such as salsa verde and dragoncella. Both salted capers and those preserved in vinegar should be rinsed well before using. The smaller salted capers have the most intense flavor.

Green bean, Parmesan

Fine green beans	**1 lb**
Parmesan	**2½ oz**
Lemon	**1**
Arugula leaves	**4 oz**
Ex. v. olive oil	

Trim the green beans. Grate the Parmesan. Squeeze the juice from the lemon. Wash and dry the arugula.

Combine the lemon juice and three times its volume of olive oil; season. Reserve 2 tbsp, and mix the rest in a warm bowl with the Parmesan.

Cook the beans in boiling salted water until tender. Drain, immediately add to the bowl, and toss well with the Parmesan. The Parmesan will melt and coat the beans. Season well.

Toss the arugula with the reserved dressing. Place on plates with the beans over; serve.

Estate-bottled extra virgin olive oil should have the name of the producer, the type of olives, the area where they were grown, and the year of production on the label. We buy Tuscan oils pressed from the Moraiolo and Frantoio olive varieties, which are picked early, thus giving the oil a fresh olive flavor, spiciness, and strong green color. As olive oil ages, it loses its intense flavor. We use young oil to pour over bruschetta, soups, salads, and vegetables, and older oil for cooking.

Green bean, mustard

Fine green beans	1 lb
Lemon	1
Flat-leaf parsley leaves	3 tbsp
Dijon mustard	3 tbsp
Ex. v. olive oil	

Trim the beans. Squeeze the juice from the lemon. Chop the parsley finely.

Cook the beans in a generous amount of salted boiling water until tender, not al dente.

Put the mustard in a bowl. Stir in the lemon juice and then very slowly add olive oil until the consistency is of mayonnaise.

Drain the beans thoroughly and add to the mustard sauce. Toss with the parsley, check seasoning, and serve while still warm.

When combining mustard in the dressing with vegetables we use a surprisingly large quantity of Dijon mustard. In this recipe its smooth texture mixed with olive oil becomes a mayonnaiselike sauce.

Cucumber, mint, mascarpone

English cucumbers	1½
Mint leaves	2 tbsp
Fresh hot red chile	1
Lemon	1
Mascarpone	1 cup
Crème fraîche	5 tbsp
Ex. v. olive oil	

Peel the cucumbers, cut in half lengthwise, and remove the seeds. Cut in half again and then into 2-inch lengths. Chop the mint. Wash the chile and finely slice on the diagonal. Squeeze the juice from the lemon.

Combine the mascarpone and crème fraîche; season well.

Combine the cucumber and mint with the lemon juice and three times its volume of olive oil. Season.

Serve with the mascarpone and the chile sprinkled over.

Look for cucumbers that are unwaxed. They should be firm and rounded to the ends. Avoid any with withered, shriveled tips or ones that bulge in the middle, because they are likely to be filled with large seeds.

Crab, fennel, tomato, radicchio

Fennel bulbs	2
Radicchio head	½
Lemons	2
Dried hot chiles	2
Flat-leaf parsley leaves	2 tbsp
Plum tomatoes	4
Ex. v. olive oil	
Crabmeat	1 lb

Remove the tough outer leaves and stems from the fennel. Remove the tough outer leaves from the radicchio. Squeeze the juice from the lemons. Crumble the chiles. Chop the parsley.

To make the salad, finely shave the fennel bulbs into a bowl. Finely slice the radicchio into the same bowl. Slice the tomatoes across as thinly as possible. Let any seeds and juice drop out. Add to the bowl.

Mix the lemon juice with four times its volume of olive oil; season. Use half this dressing to dress the salad, and mix the remainder into the crabmeat (see note) with the chile and parsley.

Serve the salad with the crabmeat alongside.

If you buy live crabs, kill them just before cooking. Put them in boiling salted water for 8 to 10 minutes, according to size, and pick the meat while the crab is still warm—it will be easier to get the meat out of the shell.

3

Salted, smoked & dried fish & meat

Bottarga, mâche salad
Smoked haddock carpaccio
Anchovy, bruschetta, butter
Smoked eel, celery, capers
Smoked eel, salicornia
Prosciutto, asparagus
Prosciutto, melon
Prosciutto, arugula
Mixed salami, two crostini
Bresaola, Parmesan, balsamic
Finocchiona salami, borlotti

Bottarga, mâche salad

Cherry tomatoes	**9 oz**
Mâche leaves	**10 oz**
Lemon	**1**
Ex. v. olive oil	
Bottarga	**7 oz**

Wash the tomatoes and cut them in half, or into quarters if larger than ¾ inch in diameter. Wash and dry the mâche. Squeeze the juice from the lemon.

Mix the lemon juice with three times its volume of olive oil; season.

Put the tomatoes and mâche together in a large salad bowl, season, and toss with the dressing. Immediately shave the bottarga over and mix in. Use a potato peeler to get fine shavings. Drizzle individual portions with olive oil.

Bottarga is the name given to the sun-dried roe of the gray mullet. Sardinia is where the fattest gray mullet are caught and where most bottarga comes from. Bottarga is sold vacuum-packed in its natural form, which is two fish roes joined. Some bottarga is dipped in wax to preserve its moisture.

Salted, smoked & dried fish & meat

Smoked haddock carpaccio

Fennel seeds	1 tbsp
Lemons	2
Smoked haddock	1½ lbs
Ex. v. olive oil	

Crush the fennel seeds. Squeeze the juice from one lemon, and cut the other into wedges.

Using a long, flat-bladed knife, slice the haddock as thinly as you possibly can along the length of the fish.

Arrange the slices to cover each plate. Sprinkle with black pepper and the fennel seeds. Drizzle the lemon juice over, then sprinkle each plate with 1 tbsp olive oil.

Serve with a wedge of lemon.

The best smoked haddock for this recipe is the Finnan haddock from the east coast of Scotland. Small haddocks are split open and the heads removed but the bones kept in, then lightly salted in brine, and finally cold smoked to a pale, straw-yellow color. Avoid bright yellow fillets of large haddock, as their flavor is too strong for carpaccio.

Salted, smoked & dried fish & meat

Anchovy, bruschetta, butter

Salted anchovies	8
Dried hot chiles	2
Lemons	3
Sourdough loaf	¼
Ex. v. olive oil	
Rosemary sprig	1 large
Unsalted butter	7 tbsp

Prepare the anchovies as in the note below. Remove the spine bones and heads. Crumble the chiles. Halve the lemons. Cut the bread into four slices.

Put the anchovy fillets on a flat plate with the juice of one lemon, black pepper, and dried chile. Drizzle olive oil over.

Grill the bread, rub with rosemary, then butter generously. Lay the anchovies on top.

Serve with lemon.

As these anchovy fillets are used whole, it is important to buy anchovies preserved in salt; those preserved in oil are more suitable for mashing or chopping. To prepare, rinse the anchovies under a slow-running cold tap to wash off residual salt. Carefully pull each fillet from the bone. Discard the head and pull off the fins and tail. Pat dry and use immediately. Or, to keep, squeeze lemon juice over and cover with olive oil. This bruschetta makes a great savory breakfast.

Salted, smoked & dried fish & meat

Smoked eel, celery, capers

Celery heads	2
Salted capers	⅓ cup
Dried hot chiles	2
Lemons	2
Ex. v. olive oil	
Smoked eel, bone in	1 lb

Pull off the tough green stalks of the celery and keep for another use. Cut the heart in half lengthwise and wash, then finely shave, keeping a few of the tender pale leaves. Rinse the capers. Crumble the chiles. Squeeze the juice from one lemon, and quarter the other.

Mix the lemon juice with three times its volume of olive oil. Season and add the chile. Put the capers in a small bowl and add 1 tbsp of the dressing. Mix the celery with the celery leaves and remaining dressing.

Skin and slice the eel, and divide among four plates. Add the celery salad and scatter the capers over. Serve with lemon.

Look for eel sold with the skin intact, as it will be fatter and juicier. The belly should be yellow and the back brown. Fat eel is definitely good eel, and the skin will peel easily.

Salted, smoked & dried fish & meat

Smoked eel, salicornia

Smoked eel, bone in	1 lb
Salicornia	14 oz
Lemons	3
Fresh horseradish	3½ oz
Crème fraîche	⅔ cup
Ex. v. olive oil	

Skin and slice the eel, and divide among four plates. Sprinkle with black pepper.

Pick through the salicornia, cutting off any tough stems. Wash thoroughly. Squeeze the juice from two of the lemons. Cut the other lemon into quarters.

Peel and finely grate the horseradish. Mix with ½ tsp sea salt and the crème fraîche. Add 2 to 3 tbsp lemon juice.

Cook the salicornia in boiling water for about 5 minutes, or until tender. Drain and toss with olive oil and 2 to 3 tbsp lemon juice.

Divide the salicornia among the plates and spoon the horseradish over. Serve with lemon wedges.

Salicornia, which is also called *marsh samphire* and *glasswort*, becomes available around the end of April. It grows along the Pacific and Atlantic coasts. Salicornia has fleshy stems and a fresh, salty taste. It is mostly sold through specialty fish merchants.

Prosciutto, asparagus

Asparagus	1 lb
Mint leaves	3 tbsp
Lemon	½
Ex. v. olive oil	
Prosciutto slices	14 oz

Preheat the oven to 425°F.

Trim the asparagus of any woody ends by flexing the base of the stalk until it snaps. Wash and dry. Chop the mint. Squeeze the juice from the lemon half.

Put the asparagus in a bowl and toss with enough olive oil to lightly coat each spear. Season.

Arrange the asparagus in a roasting pan and roast for 10 minutes.

While warm, toss the asparagus with the mint and the lemon juice. Put the prosciutto on a large plate with the asparagus.

Prosciutto, melon

Charentais, or other small, sweet melons	2
Prosciutto slices	14 oz

Halve the melons and remove the seeds.

With a large spoon, scoop out pieces from each half-melon and place on a plate. Drape the prosciutto slices over.

Prosciutto is the cured leg of pork. The curing process and aging, as well as the rearing of the pigs themselves, varies in Italy from region to region. The most famous prosciutto is from Parma, where the pigs are fed on whey, a by-product in the making of Parmesan cheese. Parma is sweet with a pale color, in contrast to prosciutto from San Daniele, which has a stronger flavor and darker color. Tuscan prosciutto is saltier than most and usually cut into thicker slices. There are many other regions that make prosciutto worth trying when visiting Italy. When buying your prosciutto, make sure it is not sliced too thin.

Salted, smoked & dried fish & meat

Prosciutto, arugula

Arugula leaves	4 oz
Red wine vinegar	1 tbsp
Dijon mustard	1 tsp
Ex. v. olive oil	3 tbsp
Prosciutto slices	14 oz

Wash the arugula carefully and dry well.

Combine the red wine vinegar and mustard. Slowly stir in the olive oil, then season.

Toss the dressing and leaves together, and place on plates in mounds. Drape the prosciutto over the arugula to cover it completely.

Use broad-leaf, cultivated arugula in this salad; it is more tender and less peppery than the small wild arugula.

There are many other varieties of arugula. Turkish, Greek, and Cypriot markets often sell bunches of a large-leaf arugula, which has a strong peppery taste and is quite fleshy. The problem is that it doesn't keep well.

We grow a Turkish variety of wild arugula. This perennial bushlike plant regrows its slender leaves each time it's picked and is the strongest-tasting arugula of all.

Mixed salami, two crostini

Felino salami	3½ oz
Finocchiona salami	3½ oz
Coppa di Parma	3½ oz
Small black olives	⅓ cup
Garlic clove	1
Dried hot chile	1
Can cannellini beans	1 (14-oz)
Ex. v. olive oil	
Ciabatta loaf	½

Finely slice the salami and coppa. Pit the olives and roughly chop. Peel the garlic and squash it with sea salt. Crumble the chile.

Drain and rinse the beans. Heat the beans in a small saucepan with the garlic salt, 3 tbsp olive oil, and some black pepper for 2 minutes, then smash roughly with a fork.

Mix the chopped olives with the chile and 1 tbsp olive oil.

Cut eight slices of ciabatta at an angle and grill on both sides. Place two slices on each plate.

Spread one crostini with the smashed cannellini and sprinkle the olives over the other. Arrange the salami and coppa alongside.

Salamis are made throughout Italy, but each region makes its own in a particular way—with different seasonings, textures, and curing, according to local customs and traditions.

The salamis we love are the lean and delicate Felino, the hard, finely chopped Milanese, and coppa, the sweet, cured, rolled shoulder from Parma. Buy salami in a piece and slice it yourself.

Salted, smoked & dried fish & meat

Bresaola, Parmesan, balsamic

Parmesan	4 oz
Lemons	1½
Ex. v. olive oil	
Bresaola slices	14 oz
Balsamic vinegar	3 tbsp

Shave the Parmesan. Squeeze the juice from the lemon half, and cut the whole lemon into wedges.

Mix the lemon juice with three times its volume of olive oil.

Place the bresaola over each plate. Season and drizzle with the lemon dressing. Cover the bresaola with the Parmesan shavings. Drizzle the balsamic over each plate.

Serve with wedges of lemon.

Bresaola is beef cured in salt and then air-dried. Like prosciutto and salami, it should be served as quickly as possible after it is sliced.

Salted, smoked & dried fish & meat

Finocchiona salami, borlotti

Fresh borlotti beans	**2¼ lbs**
Garlic cloves	**2**
Red wine vinegar	**3 tbsp**
Ex. v. olive oil	
Plum tomatoes	**4**
Finocchiona salami	**10 oz**

Pod the borlotti beans. Peel the garlic.

Put the beans in a medium-sized saucepan with the garlic and cover with water. Bring to a boil, then simmer until tender, 25 to 35 minutes. Drain and season generously, then add the vinegar and 3 tbsp olive oil.

Slice the plum tomatoes in half lengthwise, then each half into thirds lengthwise. Season the tomatoes, then mix with the borlotti beans.

Slice the salami as finely as possible. Divide the borlotti beans and tomatoes among four plates and place the salami over. Serve drizzled with olive oil.

Finocchiona is a fat, loose-textured, soft salami typical of Tuscany. Fennel seeds and garlic are combined with pork, which is then aged to develop the flavor.

Salted, smoked & dried fish & meat

Mullet Bottarga

Tomato pasta

Spaghetti, raw tomato, arugula
Tagliatelle, tomato, basil
Penne, tomato, dried porcini
Spaghetti, boiled tomato
Spaghetti, boiled tomato two
Orecchiette, tomato, ricotta
Spaghetti, tomato, green bean
Pappardelle, tomato, pancetta
Rigatoni, tomato, beef, red wine

Spaghetti, raw tomato, arugula

Plum tomatoes	4
Garlic cloves	2
Dried hot chile	1
Capers	2 tbsp
Black olives	3 tbsp
Arugula leaves	3 tbsp
Ex. v. olive oil	3 tbsp
Spaghetti	11 oz

Cut the tomatoes in half. Squeeze out excess juice and seeds, and chop the flesh coarsely. Peel the garlic and squash with 1 tsp sea salt. Crumble the chile. Rinse the capers, and pit the olives. Roughly chop the arugula.

Combine the tomatoes, garlic, chile, capers, and olives. Season generously, add the olive oil, and put aside for 30 minutes.

Cook the spaghetti in boiling salted water until al dente. Drain, and stir the pasta into the tomatoes. Add the arugula. Toss to coat each strand. Season with black pepper.

Serve with olive oil.

Plum tomatoes are fleshy and easy to peel and have hardly any juice or seeds, which makes them ideal for rich, thick tomato sauces. This raw sauce should only be made in the summer, when you can buy sun-ripened plum tomatoes that are really sweet.

Tagliatelle, tomato, basil

Garlic cloves	2
Basil leaves	2 tbsp
Parmesan	2 oz
Olive oil	1 tbsp
Can tomatoes	1 (28-oz)
Tagliatelle	11 oz
Unsalted butter	7 tbsp

Peel and slice the garlic. Tear the basil. Grate the Parmesan.

Heat the oil in a thick-bottomed pan and fry the garlic until soft but not brown. Add the tomatoes and season. Cook over medium heat for 20 to 30 minutes, or until the sauce is very thick and the oil comes to the top. Add the basil.

Cook the tagliatelle in boiling salted water until al dente. Drain in a colander. Melt half the butter in the hot pan, then return the pasta and add the remaining butter. Toss well. Add the tomato sauce and toss well again.

Serve immediately, with the Parmesan.

Plum tomatoes, in cans or jars, are an essential item in the Italian pantry. The best are the long-shaped San Marzano variety, preserved in their own juice. Avoid canned tomatoes that contain purée or sauce because this will affect the flavor of your own tomato sauce.

Penne, tomato, dried porcini

Dried porcini	1½ oz
Garlic cloves	2
Flat-leaf parsley leaves	1 tbsp
Parmesan	2 oz
Tomato sauce	5 tbsp
Unsalted butter	7 tbsp
Penne	11 oz
Ex. v. olive oil	

Soak the porcini in 1 cup of boiling-hot water for 10 minutes. Peel and finely slice the garlic. Chop the parsley. Grate the Parmesan. Make the tomato sauce (see page 62).

Drain the porcini, straining the liquid through cheesecloth or a paper towel into a bowl. Rinse the porcini and chop coarsely.

In a thick-bottomed saucepan, melt the butter and add the garlic. Add the porcini and fry until soft. Add a little of the porcini liquid and simmer until it has been absorbed. Stir in the chopped parsley. Add the tomato sauce and season.

Cook the penne in boiling salted water until al dente. Drain and stir the pasta into the sauce. Toss well.

Drizzle with olive oil and serve with grated Parmesan.

This sauce is best served with a hard pasta, such as penne. It is also delicious with wet polenta. When buying dried porcini, look for pale-colored stems and light brown caps, as darker pieces may have been oven-dried. A fresh, light porcini perfume (as opposed to a strong yeastlike smell) is also a good indicator.

Spaghetti, boiled tomato

Ripe plum tomatoes	1 lb
Red onion	1
Carrot	1
Celery head	½
Basil leaves	2 tbsp
Dried hot chile	1
Can tomatoes	1 (14-oz)
Spaghetti	11 oz
Ex. v. olive oil	

Make a slit in the side of each tomato, put in a bowl, and cover with boiling water. Leave for ½ minute, then remove into cold water. Peel as soon as the tomatoes are cool enough to touch; chop. Peel the onion and cut in half. Wash the carrot and cut in half. Remove the outer stalks of the celery, and use the white part. Wash and chop the basil, and crumble the chile.

Put all the vegetables into a saucepan with the canned tomatoes, season, and bring to a boil. Simmer gently for 45 minutes, or until the vegetables are soft and some of the juices have evaporated. Cool, then put through a food mill. Stir in the basil and chile.

Cook the spaghetti in boiling salted water until al dente, drain, and add to the sauce.

Serve with olive oil.

To preserve tomatoes, choose ripe, unblemished tomatoes. Blanch and peel them, then pack tightly into sterilized jars and seal loosely. Put the jars in the oven at 400°F., or into a large pan of boiling water, and process for 20 minutes. Alternatively, blanch and peel, remove seeds, and chop the flesh. Boil for 5 minutes, then pack into sterilized jars and hermetically seal.

Spaghetti, boiled tomato two

Ripe plum tomatoes	4½ lbs
Red onion	½
Basil leaves	2 tbsp
Spaghetti	11 oz
Ex. v. olive oil	

To make a tomato purée, make a slit in the side of each tomato. Bring a large saucepan of water to a boil and add 1 tbsp sea salt. Add the tomatoes and leave them in the water until the water comes back to a boil.

Remove the tomatoes with a slotted spoon and peel off the skins while still warm. Make a cut into the length of each tomato, and put in a colander over a bowl to drain off all the juices. Leave for 1 hour. Put the tomato pulp through a food mill. Bottle if not using immediately.

To make the sauce, peel and grate the onion on the coarse side of the grater. Chop the basil.

Put the onion into a medium-sized, thick-bottomed saucepan and cover with ¾ inch water. Heat gently and simmer until all the water has evaporated. Add the tomato purée and 2 tsp sea salt. Simmer for 20 minutes, or until the sauce is thick and sweet. Season.

Cook the spaghetti in boiling salted water until al dente, then drain and add to the sauce. Add the basil and olive oil.

Both of these tomato sauces are made without olive oil in the base. The oil is added only at the end. This recipe was given to us by the Planeta family of Sicily.

Orecchiette, tomato, ricotta

Cherry tomatoes	12 oz
Garlic clove	1
Parmesan	2 oz
Basil leaves	3 tbsp
Ex. v. olive oil	1 tbsp
Ricotta	scant 1 cup
Orecchiette	11 oz

Cut the tomatoes in half and squeeze out the juice and seeds. Peel and finely chop the garlic. Grate the Parmesan. Wash the basil.

Combine the tomatoes and garlic, season, add the oil, and toss to combine. Let marinate for 15 minutes. Put the ricotta in a bowl, season, and stir.

Cook the orecchiette in boiling salted water until al dente, then drain.

Gently heat the tomato mixture and add the drained orecchiette, stirring gently to combine. Finally, stir in the ricotta.

Serve with the Parmesan.

Orecchiette—little ears—is the pasta of Puglia. The tomatoes for this recipe should be almost over-ripe. Ricotta is tossed in at the end and coats the orecchiette, clinging to the hollows of the pasta.

Spaghetti, tomato, green bean

Garlic cloves	2
Dried hot chile	1
Parmesan	2 oz
Ex. v. olive oil	1 tbsp
Can tomatoes	1 (14-oz)
Fine green beans	4 oz
Spaghetti	11 oz

Peel and finely slice the garlic. Crumble the chile. Grate the Parmesan.

Heat a thick-bottomed pan. Add the olive oil, then the garlic, and cook until soft but not brown. Add the canned tomatoes, season, and add the chile. Cook over medium heat for 20 minutes.

Trim the green beans, then cook in boiling salted water until very tender. Drain well. Combine the beans with the tomato sauce.

Cook the spaghetti in boiling salted water until al dente. Drain and stir the pasta into the tomato and green beans. Season and toss with a little olive oil.

Serve with the Parmesan.

Vegetables, cooked until soft and then combined with thick tomato sauce, are typical of southern Italian cooking. We were excited by this combination of green beans, tomato, and spaghetti. The green beans should be incredibly fine so they will twirl around the fork with the spaghetti.

Pappardelle, tomato, pancetta

Plum tomatoes	6
Pancetta slices	5 oz
Dried hot chiles	2
Parmesan	3½ oz
Unsalted butter	10 tbsp
Heavy cream	⅔ cup
Egg pappardelle	11 oz

Peel the tomatoes (see page 66), rei
seeds, and roughly chop the flesh. Cu
pancetta into ¾-inch pieces. Crumble ι
chiles, and grate the Parmesan.

Melt the butter in a thick-bottomed pan, adc
the pancetta and chile, and gently cook until
the pancetta begins to color. Add the tomato,
season, and cook gently for 10 minutes. Add
the cream and cook for 10 minutes longer.

Cook the pappardelle in boiling salted water
until al dente. Drain and add to the sauce. Stir
in half the Parmesan.

Serve with the remaining Parmesan.

Pancetta is cured belly of pork, either salted
and dried (stesa) or smoked (affumicata).
Pancetta stesa is sometimes cured with herbs
such as rosemary and/or black pepper.
Pancetta affumicata is usually leaner and
should be cut finer, as it can be tough.

We try to use a fatty stesa in this recipe, slowly
cooked to release its delicious juices.

When choosing pancetta, look for even layers
of fat and meat and a sweet perfume—a porky
smell indicates lack of aging and will affect the
flavor of the sauce.

Tomato pasta

Rigatoni, tomato, beef, red wine

Beef tenderloin	1 (7-oz)
Garlic cloves	4
Parmesan	2 oz
Unsalted butter	7 tbsp
Cans tomatoes	1½ (14-oz)
Chianti wine	1½ cups
Ground black pepper	1 tbsp
Ex. v. olive oil	3 tbsp
Rigatoni	11 oz

Trim the tenderloin and cut across into ¼-inch-thick slices. Cut the slices into ½-inch strips. Peel and slice the garlic. Grate the Parmesan.

Heat the butter in a thick-bottomed pan, add the garlic, and fry gently until brown. Add the tomatoes and season. Cook over high heat for 5 minutes, stirring to break up the tomatoes, then add half the red wine. Continue to cook quite fast, adding more wine as the sauce reduces. Cook for a total of 15 minutes, using up all the wine, then stir in the pepper.

Heat the olive oil in a skillet until very hot. Add the beef pieces and fry very briefly, just to brown each piece on both sides. Stir the beef into the sauce with any juices from the pan.

Cook the rigatoni in boiling salted water until al dente. Drain and add to the sauce.

Serve with the Parmesan.

Red wine is traditionally added to meat-based sauces. Here, the wine is reduced with the tomatoes before the beef is added. In sausage sauces from Tuscany, the wine is cooked with the sausage to soften and sweeten the flavor. All'Amatriciana is the Roman sauce in which red wine is added to the crisp onion and pancetta base used to flavor the tomato.

Tomato pasta

5

Fish pasta

Linguine, sardine, saffron
Bucatini, sardine, salted anchovy
Orecchiette, scallop, arugula
Spaghetti, squid, zucchini
Taglierini, clam, fried zucchini
Ditaloni, mussels, white wine
Tagliatelle, langoustine, ricotta
Orecchiette, clam, broccoli
Tagliatelle, shrimp, pea
Linguine, clam, white asparagus
Spaghetti, roasted red mullet
Tagliatelle, zucchini, mullet
Linguine, crab

Linguine, sardine, saffron

Sardines	12
Garlic cloves	2
Flat-leaf parsley leaves	2 tbsp
Dried hot chiles	2
Saffron threads	½ tsp
Raisins	⅓ cup
Lemon	1
Ex. v. olive oil	
Pine nuts	⅓ cup
Linguine	11 oz

Fillet the sardines. Peel and finely slice the garlic. Chop the parsley, and crumble the chiles. Sprinkle the saffron threads over 3 tbsp of hot water and let stand for 20 minutes. Soak the raisins in warm water for 20 minutes. Cut the lemon into quarters.

Heat 3 tbsp olive oil in a heavy-bottomed skillet and fry the garlic and parsley. Add the sardine fillets in one layer and fry gently for 2 minutes, or until cooked through, spooning the garlic and parsley over them. Season.

In a separate skillet, brown the pine nuts, then sprinkle with the chile.

Cook the linguine in boiling salted water until al dente; drain and return to the pot. Drain the raisins and add to the pasta with the saffron. Toss to combine. Add the sardines and juices from the pan, and check the seasoning. Scatter the pine nuts and chile over. Serve drizzled with olive oil and lemon juice.

Pasta with sardines is one of the classic dishes of Sicily. As in any beloved regional recipe, the ingredients vary from cook to cook. This version includes the traditional pine nuts and raisins, but has the addition of saffron. Buy the threads, not the powder; the color should be deep orange.

Fish pasta

Bucatini, sardine, salted anchovy

Sardines	12
Red onion	1
Garlic cloves	2
Salted anchovies	4
Fennel seeds	1 tbsp
Dried hot chiles	2
Capers	⅓ cup
Ex. v. olive oil	
Can tomatoes	1 (14-oz)
White wine	⅔ cup
Bucatini	11 oz

Fillet the sardines. Peel and finely slice the onion and garlic. Wash the anchovies free of salt, fillet, and roughly chop. Grind the fennel seeds. Crumble the chiles. Rinse the capers.

Heat 1 tbsp olive oil in a small, thick-bottomed pan. Add half the garlic and fry until golden, then add the tomatoes and salt. Simmer for 20 minutes.

Heat 2 tbsp olive oil in a large, flat, thick-bottomed skillet. Gently fry the onion until soft and beginning to color. Add the anchovies, the remaining garlic, the fennel seeds, and chile, and cook together to melt the anchovy and soften the garlic.

Lay the sardine fillets in one layer over this mixture. Spoon on 3 to 4 tbsp of the tomato sauce and season generously. Pour in the wine and sprinkle with the capers, then cover and cook for 3 to 4 minutes, or until the sardines are cooked and the wine has mixed with the sauce.

Cook the bucatini in boiling salted water until al dente. Drain and add to the sardines. Toss together in the pan over heat. Check for seasoning.

Serve with olive oil drizzled over.

Orecchiette, scallop, arugula

Sea scallops	8
Arugula leaves	4 oz
Cherry tomatoes	1 lb
Garlic cloves	2
Fresh hot red chiles	2
Lemon	1
Ex. v. olive oil	
Orecchiette	11 oz

Cut the scallops into quarters. Wash, dry, and chop the arugula. Cut the tomatoes in half and squeeze out the seeds and juice. Peel and finely chop the garlic. Cut the chiles in half lengthwise, scrape out the seeds, and finely chop. Cut the lemon into four wedges.

Put the tomato pieces in a bowl and add the chile, garlic, and 2 tbsp olive oil. Season generously and put aside.

Heat 1 tbsp olive oil in a thick-bottomed skillet and add the scallops. Season and fry briefly until brown, then stir in the marinated tomatoes. Cook only briefly, just to combine.

Cook the orecchiette in boiling salted water until al dente, then drain and add to the skillet. Stir in the arugula and test for seasoning.

Serve drizzled with olive oil, with a squeeze of lemon.

Spaghetti, squid, zucchini

Squid	1 lb
Zucchini	14 oz
Garlic cloves	2
Dried hot chile	1
Lemon	1
Ex. v. olive oil	
Marjoram leaves	2 tbsp
Spaghetti	11 oz

Prepare the squid by pulling away the head and tentacles from the body. Cut off the tentacles and squeeze out the beak. Open the body out into a flat piece and scrape away the soft interior pulp. Finely slice the body. Separate the tentacles. Wash and pat dry.

Wash the zucchini and grate at an angle on the large side of a cheese grater. Sprinkle with salt and put in a colander to drain for 15 minutes. Wash off the salt and pat dry.

Peel and finely slice the garlic. Crumble the chile. Grate the zest of the lemon finely, then squeeze out the juice.

Heat a large, thick-bottomed skillet, add 3 tbsp olive oil, and, when smoking hot, add the squid. Stir briefly, then add salt, pepper, and chile, followed by the zucchini and garlic. Stir-fry just to brown the squid and soften the zucchini. Add the lemon juice and zest and the marjoram; stir. Remove from the heat.

Cook the spaghetti in boiling salted water, then drain and add to the squid mixture. Toss.

Serve drizzled with olive oil.

Taglierini, clam, fried zucchini

Clams	2¼ lbs
Zucchini	1 lb
Garlic clove	1
Flat-leaf parsley leaves	1 tbsp
Dried hot chile	1
Ex. v. olive oil	
White wine	1 cup
Unsalted butter	2 tbsp
Taglierini	11 oz

Wash the clams. Trim the ends off the zucchini and slice as finely as possible into disks. Peel and finely chop the garlic. Finely chop the parsley. Crumble the chile.

In a thick-bottomed pan, heat 1 tbsp olive oil. Fry the garlic and chile for 1 minute, then add the clams and white wine. Cover and cook over high heat until the clams open, about 3 minutes. Drain, reserving the liquid. Take the clams out of the shells and discard the shells.

Return the clam liquid to the pan and boil to reduce by half. Lower the heat and stir in the butter and parsley.

Heat 5 tbsp olive oil in a heavy-bottomed skillet and cook the zucchini in one layer until lightly browned on both sides. Drain on paper towels. Season.

Cook the taglierini in boiling salted water until al dente. Drain and add to the sauce, along with the clams. Toss well.

Serve with the zucchini on top.

Ditaloni, mussels, white wine

Mussels	2¼ lbs
Garlic cloves	2
Flat-leaf parsley leaves	4 tbsp
Unsalted butter	14 tbsp
Ex. v. olive oil	1 tbsp
White wine	½ cup
Heavy cream	⅔ cup
Ditaloni	11 oz

Scrub the mussels. Peel and finely chop the garlic. Finely chop the parsley.

Heat half the butter with the oil, then add the garlic and mussels. Pour in the wine; season, then cover and cook over high heat until the mussels open. Drain the mussels, keeping the cooking liquid. Remove the mussels from the shells; discard the shells and any mussels that haven't opened.

Heat the remaining butter in a pan and add the mussel juices and the cream. Cook gently to reduce to a rich, creamy consistency. Then add the mussels and parsley.

Cook the ditaloni in boiling salted water until al dente, then drain and add to the sauce. Toss together over low heat, and serve.

Ditaloni is a small, tubular pasta. Cavatelle or short penne can be used as an alternative. Buy small mussels so they are the same size as the pasta.

Tagliatelle, langoustine, ricotta

Lemons	2
Dried hot chile	1
Ricotta	1½ cups
Ex. v. olive oil	
Langoustines	4½ lbs
Tagliatelle	11 oz
Basil leaves	3 tbsp

Grate the zest from one lemon and squeeze out the juice. Cut the other lemon into wedges. Crumble the chile.

Lightly beat the ricotta and add half of the lemon juice and all the zest, then stir in 3 tbsp olive oil. Season generously.

Cook the langoustines in boiling salted water for 2 minutes. Drain and peel off the shells. Cut each in half lengthwise. Season while warm, and drizzle with a little oil and lemon juice.

Cook the tagliatelle in boiling salted water until al dente, then drain and stir into the ricotta. Add the langoustines and the basil torn into pieces.

Serve with wedges of lemon.

We first encountered this idea of combining fish and ricotta at the famous restaurant Romano in Viareggio. In this recipe, the light creaminess of the ricotta with the freshly boiled langoustines makes a unique summer pasta.

Orecchiette, clam, broccoli

Clams	2¼ lbs
Broccoli	10 oz
Garlic cloves	3
Fresh hot red chile	1
Flat-leaf parsley leaves	1 tbsp
Dried hot chile	1
Ex. v. olive oil	
Anchovy fillets	3
White wine	⅔ cup
Orecchiette	11 oz

Wash the clams. Cut the flowerets from the broccoli head; discard the big stalks. Cut each floweret in half lengthwise. Peel and finely chop the garlic. Remove seeds from the fresh chile, then chop. Chop the parsley. Crumble the dried chile.

Cook the broccoli in boiling salted water until very tender; drain.

Heat 2 tbsp olive oil in a thick-bottomed pan. Add half the garlic and fry until soft, then add the anchovies and dried chile. Stir to melt the anchovies. Add the broccoli and cook for 10 minutes, or until it breaks up to make a sauce.

Heat 2 tbsp olive oil in a large pan. Add the fresh chile, remaining garlic, and the parsley, and fry until just brown. Add the clams and wine, cover, and cook over high heat until the clams open, about 3 minutes. Drain, reserving the liquid.

Remove the clams from their shells and add to the broccoli with enough of their cooking liquid to make the sauce thinner.

Cook the orecchiette in boiling salted water until al dente. Drain and add to the sauce, stirring well to combine and adding more liquid as necessary.

Serve with olive oil.

Tagliatelle, shrimp, pea

Garlic cloves	2
Mint leaves	2 tbsp
Lemon	1
Unsalted butter	10 tbsp
Shelled small shrimp	10 oz
Frozen peas	1 lb
Tagliatelle	11 oz

Peel and finely chop the garlic. Coarsely chop the mint. Squeeze the juice from the lemon.

Melt half the butter in a thick-bottomed pan and add the garlic. Fry until soft, then add the shrimp. Stir to combine, then season and add half the lemon juice.

Cook the peas until tender in boiling salted water. Drain and add to the shrimp.

Cook the tagliatelle in boiling salted water until al dente. Drain and add to the shrimp and peas. Add the mint and the remaining butter and lemon juice. Toss well, then check the seasoning and serve.

We use small, cold water brown shrimp—the same as those found in traditional English potted shrimp. You can still collect these brown shrimp at low tide around the sandy coasts and estuaries of Britain. Use the smallest shrimp you can find.

Linguine, clam, white asparagus

Clams	2¼ lbs
White asparagus	1 lb
Cinnamon stick	1 (1¼-inch)
Parmesan	2 oz
Unsalted butter	14 tbsp
White wine	½ cup
Linguine	11 oz

Wash the clams. Snap off the tough ends of the asparagus and peel the stalks, then cut each spear lengthwise into fine ribbons. Break up the cinnamon. Grate the Parmesan.

Heat half the butter gently in a large, heavy-bottomed pan. Add the cinnamon, clams, and wine; season. Cover and cook over high heat to open the clams, about 3 minutes. Drain, reserving the liquid. Remove half of the clam shells. Return the clams to the liquid.

Cook the linguine in boiling salted water for 6 minutes, then add the asparagus and cook together until the pasta is al dente. Drain and return to the pan. Add the remaining butter and the clams and their juices. Check for seasoning.

Serve with Parmesan.

The combination of white asparagus, butter, and cinnamon as a pasta sauce for clams was introduced to us in Verona's famous fish restaurant, Osteria all'Oste Scuro.

Spaghetti, roasted red mullet

Red mullet	2 (1-lb)
Small black olives	⅔ cup
Dried hot chiles	2
Cherry tomatoes	14 oz
Ex. v. olive oil	
Thyme leaves	1 tbsp
Spaghetti	11 oz

Ask your fish merchant to fillet the mullet.

Preheat the oven to 400°F.

Pit the olives. Crumble the chiles.

Toss the cherry tomatoes with a little olive oil. Season and put in a baking pan in one layer. Prick each with a fork. Roast in the preheated oven for 20 minutes.

Place the mullet fillets in one layer in a shallow baking dish, and sprinkle with thyme and chile; season. Drizzle with olive oil and roast in the preheated oven for 5 minutes.

Cook the spaghetti in boiling salted water until al dente. Drain and return to the pan.

Add the olives and tomatoes to the pasta with 1 tbsp olive oil and season. Add the mullet and toss gently. Serve.

Red mullet has a strong flavor and firm flesh, so it will stay intact when tossed with the olives, tomatoes, and spaghetti. It is the most perishable of fish and should be eaten the day it is bought.

Tagliatelle, zucchini, mullet

Red mullet	4 (12-oz)
Zucchini	1 lb
Garlic cloves	3
Plum tomatoes	6
Lemons	2
Ex. v. olive oil	
Basil leaves	3 tbsp
Egg tagliatelle	11 oz

Ask the fish merchant to fillet the mullet. Slice the fillets across into ½-inch pieces. Wash the zucchini and grate at an angle on the coarse side of the grater. Put in a colander and scatter 1 tbsp sea salt over. Leave for 15 minutes, then squeeze dry. Peel the garlic and cut into fine slivers. Peel the tomatoes (see page 66), then roughly chop. Squeeze the juice from one lemon; quarter the other.

Heat 1 tsp oil in a thick-bottomed pan, add the garlic, and brown lightly. Add the tomatoes and half of the basil; season with sea salt. Cook for 15 minutes.

Cook the tagliatelle with the zucchini in boiling salted water until al dente. Drain.

Add the mullet pieces to the hot tomato sauce and pour in the lemon juice. Season the fish, then stir to combine. Mix the tagliatelle and zucchini into the sauce, and add the remaining basil leaves.

Serve with the lemon quarters and a drizzle of olive oil.

Fish pasta

Linguine, crab

Fennel bulb	1
Garlic clove	1
Fennel seeds	1 tbsp
Dried hot chiles	2
Lemon	1
Ex. v. olive oil	
Crabmeat	14 oz
Linguine	11 oz

Remove the tough outer part and stem from the fennel. Slice the bulb across the grain as finely as you can. Keep the green tops. Peel and finely chop the garlic. Crush the fennel seeds, and crumble the chiles. Grate the zest from the lemon, and squeeze out the juice.

Heat 2 tbsp oil in a thick-bottomed pan, add the garlic, fennel seeds, and chile, and cook to soften. Add the crab, lemon zest, and juice; season. Stir through, just to heat up the crab.

Cook the linguine in boiling salted water for 5 minutes, then add the fennel slices and cook together until al dente. Drain the pasta, keeping a little of the water, and add to the crab mixture. Stir thoroughly to combine, adding a little of the reserved water to loosen the sauce, if necessary.

Serve with olive oil.

If cooking crab yourself, buy them alive and choose one or two large crabs—it will be easier to pick the meat out of these than from many small ones.

Spider crabs are very sweet and good for this recipe, although it takes longer to pick out the meat than other crabs, as the meat-to-shell ratio is less.

Fish pasta

6

Really easy soups

Asparagus, prosciutto
Tomato, chickpea, sage
Bread, tomato, basil, cucumber
Borlotti bean, pappardelle
Chickpea, pork
Savoy cabbage, ricotta crostini
Pea, zucchini
Mushroom, barley
Pumpkin, mascarpone
Rice, chestnut
Broccoli, red wine

Asparagus, prosciutto

Asparagus	1 lb
Prosciutto slices	5 oz
Red onion	1
Medium potatoes	2
Spinach	5 oz
Bouillon cubes	2
Flat-leaf parsley leaves	2 tbsp
Ex. v. olive oil	

Remove the tough ends from the asparagus, and cut the remainder of the stalks into 1-inch lengths. Keep the tips to one side. Slice the prosciutto into ribbons. Peel and chop the onion. Peel the potatoes and cut into ½-inch cubes. Wash the spinach. Dissolve the bouillon cubes in 3 cups of boiling water. Chop the parsley.

Heat 2 tbsp oil in a thick-bottomed pan, add the onion, and soften for 5 minutes, then add the prosciutto, potatoes, parsley, and asparagus stalks. Season and cook for 5 minutes, stirring, then add the bouillon and simmer until the potatoes and asparagus are tender, about 15 minutes. Add the spinach and the asparagus tips and cook for 3 minutes longer. Remove from the heat and blend the soup to a rough purée, keeping a few of the tips aside.

Heat 3 tbsp olive oil and fry the reserved tips just for a few seconds. Serve the soup with the tips and the oil they were fried in drizzled over each bowl.

Tomato, chickpea, sage

Dried chickpeas	1 cup
Baking soda	1 tsp
All-purpose flour	1 tsp
Celery stalks	2
Can tomatoes	1 (14-oz)
Garlic cloves	3
Sage leaves	8
Ex. v. olive oil	
Ditaloni	1 cup

Soak the chickpeas overnight with the baking soda and flour. Drain and rinse. Put the chickpeas into a thick-bottomed saucepan, cover with water, and add the celery. Bring to a boil, skim, and simmer for 35 to 40 minutes, or until soft. Drain and season. Drain the tomatoes of their juices, and roughly chop. Peel the garlic and finely slice. Chop the sage.

Heat 2 tbsp olive oil in a thick-bottomed pan and fry the garlic and sage together for 2 to 3 minutes. Add the chickpeas, chopped tomatoes, salt, and pepper, and stir. Bring to a simmer, then cook for 20 minutes.

Cook the pasta in boiling salted water until al dente, then drain. Toss with olive oil and seasoning.

In a food processor, pulse-chop the chickpea mixture. It should be very thick.

Stir the pasta into the soup, and serve with olive oil stirred into each portion.

This soup is from the Capezzana wine and olive oil estate in Carmignano near Florence. They make it there at the beginning of November to show off their newly pressed, beautifully spicy, and thick, green olive oil.

Bread, tomato, basil, cucumber

Tomatoes	4
English cucumber	1
Garlic clove	1
Fresh hot red chiles	2
Ciabatta slices	4
Red wine vinegar	¼ cup
Ex. v. olive oil	
Basil leaves	¼ cup

Peel the tomatoes (see page 66), cut in half, and squeeze out the seeds. Chop the flesh to a pulp and put in a bowl. Peel the cucumber, cut in half and halve again lengthwise, then cut out the seeds. Chop the flesh finely. Peel and finely chop the garlic with 1 tsp sea salt. Cut the chiles in half lengthwise, scrape out the seeds, and finely chop. Add the cucumber, garlic, and chiles to the tomatoes.

Soak the ciabatta slices in a little cold water so they are thoroughly moist. Sprinkle with the vinegar and leave for 10 minutes.

Squeeze out the bread and chop finely. Stir into the tomato mixture. Add black pepper and 3 tbsp olive oil and mix thoroughly.

Tear the basil into small pieces and stir into the soup. Serve with more olive oil.

The Tuscan tradition of adding bread to soups is exemplified by the Florentine soup Pappa Pomodoro. We have four different recipes in our previous books. This is a light, uncooked version and very easy to make.

Borlotti bean, pappardelle

Fresh borlotti beans	**2¼ lbs**
Potatoes	**7 oz**
Parsley leaves	**1 tbsp**
Sage leaves	**1 tbsp**
Rosemary leaves	**8**
Garlic cloves	**2**
Pancetta slices	**4 oz**
Ex. v. olive oil	
Pappardelle	**2 oz**

Pod the borlotti beans. Peel the potatoes and cut into ⅛-inch cubes. Finely chop the parsley, sage, and rosemary. Peel and finely chop the garlic. Cut the pancetta into fine matchsticks.

In a thick-bottomed saucepan, heat 2 tbsp olive oil, add the chopped herbs and garlic, and fry gently for 5 minutes. Add the pancetta and cook until soft, then stir in the potatoes and beans. Add enough hot water to cover, bring to a boil, and cook until the beans are soft, about half an hour. Season.

Put the mixture into a food processor and blend until thick. Return to the saucepan.

Just before serving, cook the pappardelle in boiling salted water until al dente. Drain and add to the soup.

Serve with olive oil.

Almost every region in Italy has versions of bean soup. This version from Milan uses pappardelle, a fresh, wide, ribbon egg pasta. In Venice, it is made with small, dried tubular pasta.

Chickpea, pork

Dried chickpeas	1 cup
Baking soda	1 tsp
Fresh pork belly	1 lb
Celery head	1
Medium potatoes	2
Carrot	1
Bay leaf	1
Ex. v. olive oil	

Soak the dried chickpeas overnight, adding the baking soda to the water.

Cut the pork belly into 2-inch pieces. Wash the celery and discard the outer stalks; cut the pale heart into quarters. Peel the potatoes and cut into ½-inch cubes. Wash and halve the carrot.

Drain the chickpeas and rinse in cold water. Put into a thick-bottomed saucepan with the pork, vegetables, and bay leaf. Just cover with water and bring to a boil, skimming if necessary. Turn down the heat and simmer gently for about 2 hours, or until the pork is soft.

Break up the cooked vegetables into the chickpea liquid with a fork; season generously.

Serve with a drizzle of olive oil.

This is a very basic soup, which we ate in Masuelli, a restaurant in Milan. The broth is simply the cooking water of the combined ingredients.

Savoy cabbage, ricotta crostini

Savoy cabbage	½
Garlic clove	1
Parmesan	2 oz
Chicken bouillon cubes	3
Ricotta	½ cup
Ex. v. olive oil	
Ciabatta slices	4

Remove the tough outer leaves from the cabbage; core. Slice the cabbage and wash thoroughly. Peel the garlic, and grate the Parmesan. Dissolve the bouillon cubes in 4 cups of boiling water.

Mix the ricotta with 1 tbsp olive oil; season.

Bring the bouillon to a boil, add the cabbage, and cook until very tender.

Toast the ciabatta slices and lightly rub with garlic. Drizzle lightly with olive oil and put a spoonful of ricotta on top, pressing gently into the surface.

Place one crostini in each soup bowl. Spoon the cabbage over, then ladle in the bouillon.

Drizzle olive oil over and serve sprinkled with Parmesan.

Good-quality bouillon cubes are an easy alternative to homemade broth. Italians would make their own broth with a stewing hen, celery, carrots, parsley, and onion, boiled for 2 to 2½ hours. Traditionally, clear soups include either pasta or crostini to make them more of a meal.

Really easy soups

Pea, zucchini

Zucchini	1 lb
Garlic cloves	2
Parmesan	2 oz
Bouillon cubes	2
Ex. v. olive oil	
Podded fresh peas	3½ cups
Basil leaves	3 tbsp

Trim the ends from the zucchini; cut them in half lengthwise and then across into ½-inch pieces. Peel and chop the garlic. Grate the Parmesan. Dissolve the bouillon cubes in 3 cups of boiling water.

In a thick-bottomed saucepan, heat 2 tbsp olive oil and fry the garlic until soft. Add the zucchini and cook, stirring, until soft. Add half the peas, stir, and then add half the bouillon. Cook until the peas are tender. Put into a food processor and pulse-chop to a coarse purée.

Bring the remaining peas to a boil in the remaining bouillon and cook for 5 minutes. Scoop out the peas with a slotted spoon and stir into the soup, adding a little of the bouillon if the soup is too thick.

Serve with torn basil leaves and grated Parmesan.

Italian soups are distinctly thick—in this recipe we pulse-chop the cooked vegetables in a food processor and add more peas at the end. Frozen petite peas work just as well.

Mushroom, barley

Pearl barley	6 tbsp
Dried porcini	1¼ oz
Cremini mushrooms	12 oz
Medium potatoes	7 oz
Red onion	1
Garlic cloves	2
Parsley leaves	1 tbsp
Sage leaves	1 tbsp
Bouillon cubes	2
Bay leaf	1
Ex. v. olive oil	
Can tomatoes	½ (14-oz)

Cook the barley in plenty of water for 1 hour or until soft, then drain.

Soak the porcini in 1 cup of boiling water for about 10 minutes. Chop the cremini mushrooms coarsely, and peel and cut the potatoes into ⅛-inch cubes. Peel and finely chop the onion and garlic, and finely chop the parsley and sage.

Drain the porcini, reserving the liquid; strain it through cheesecloth. Rinse the porcini and chop. Dissolve the bouillon cubes in 3 cups of boiling water and add the bay leaf.

In a heavy-bottomed saucepan, heat 3 tbsp olive oil. Add half the garlic, all the onion, and the herbs and cook until soft. Add the potatoes and stir until they are lightly browned. Stir in the tomatoes and add the bouillon and the porcini liquid. Simmer until all the vegetables are very soft.

Heat 2 tbsp olive oil in a skillet and fry the remaining garlic and the porcini until soft. Add the cremini mushrooms, season, and cook for 10 minutes longer, or until dark.

Mix the barley and mushrooms into the soup. Serve with a drizzle of olive oil.

Pumpkin, mascarpone

Pumpkin	1 (1¾-lb)
Medium potatoes	3
Garlic cloves	3
Fennel seeds	1 tsp
Plum tomatoes	9 oz
Bouillon cubes	2
Parmesan	2 oz
Mascarpone	⅔ cup
Ex. v. olive oil	

Peel the pumpkin, remove the seeds, and cut into ¾-inch cubes. Peel the potatoes and cut into ¾-inch cubes. Peel the garlic, and grind the fennel seeds. Peel the tomatoes (see page 66). Dissolve the bouillon cubes in 2 cups of boiling water. Grate the Parmesan.

Put the potatoes, tomatoes, pumpkin, and garlic cloves into a saucepan and just cover with the bouillon. Season and add the fennel seeds. Simmer for 30 minutes, or until the vegetables are tender.

Mash the soup with a potato masher—it should be thick and creamy.

Serve with spoonfuls of mascarpone, olive oil, and Parmesan.

Pumpkins taste better when they are really ripe; the flesh should be close-textured and deep orange, the seeds plump. Butternut squash can be used instead, and canned tomatoes, drained of excess juice, can replace the fresh tomatoes.

Rice, chestnut

Chestnuts	1 lb
Can borlotti beans	1 (14-oz)
Pancetta slices	4 oz
Rosemary sprig	1
Bouillon cube	1
Parmesan	2½ oz
Unsalted butter	2 tbsp
Risotto rice	¼ cup
Milk	7 fl oz

To remove the skins from the chestnuts, make a shallow cut in each and place in a saucepan. Cover with water and boil for 15 minutes. Peel off the skins while the chestnuts are still hot. Roughly chop.

Drain and rinse the borlotti beans. Cut the pancetta into matchsticks. Finely chop the rosemary. Dissolve the bouillon cube in 2 cups of boiling water. Grate the Parmesan.

Heat the butter gently in a thick-bottomed saucepan, add the pancetta and rosemary, and cook for 10 minutes to blend the flavors. Add the chestnuts, stir to coat with butter, and cook for a few more minutes. Add the rice, stirring it into the mixture, then slowly add the bouillon. As the rice begins to plump up, absorbing the bouillon, add the milk. Cook for 20 minutes longer, or until both the rice and chestnuts are soft.

Stir in the borlotti beans and more milk if too thick. Season; serve with Parmesan.

Substitute frozen chestnuts for fresh to save time. Canned chestnuts are also good. You would need two 14-oz cans for this recipe.

Really easy soups

Broccoli, red wine

Broccoli rabe	1¾ lbs
Garlic clove	1
Lambrusco red wine	3 cups
Ex. v. olive oil	

Cut the spears from the broccoli heads. Discard the big stalks. Remove the bigger and tougher leaves. Cut each spear of broccoli in two. Peel and cut the garlic in half.

Put the broccoli and garlic into a medium-sized, thick-bottomed saucepan, then add enough wine to half cover the broccoli. Add a similar quantity of water so the broccoli is completely covered. Season, then cover the pan and simmer for 20 minutes.

Serve with a drizzle of olive oil.

La Latteria is a tiny, family-run restaurant situated in an old dairy in the market in Milan, with just a few shared tables and wonderful, simple, original food. This seasonal soup, using broccoli rabe and young, local red wine, such as Lambrusco, is surprisingly delicious. Choose leafy purple broccoli rabe and include the small leaves in the soup.

7

Fish with . . .

Baked bass in the bag, fennel
Sea bass baked in sea salt
Poached turbot, salsa verde
Sea bass, potato, tomato
Langoustine, sea salt, olive oil
Grilled red mullet, crostini
Raw tuna, bruschetta
Fried scallop, borlotti
Crab, chile, fennel

Baked bass in the bag, fennel

Sea bass	1 (4½-lb)
Fennel bulbs	2
Lemons	2
Dried hot chiles	2
Unsalted butter	14 tbsp
Extra-dry vermouth	⅔ cup

Ask your fish merchant to scale and fillet the sea bass. Divide each fillet in half to make four portions.

Preheat the oven to 400°F.

Remove the tough outer stems and leaves from the fennel and slice lengthwise, keeping the green tops. Finely grate the zest and squeeze the juice from one lemon; cut the second lemon into quarters. Crumble the chiles. Soften half of the butter.

Cook the fennel in boiling salted water for 4 minutes; drain and let cool.

To make the bags, cut foil into four 2 by 20-inch lengths. Fold over to make 10-inch squares. Smear each generously with soft butter; season. Place a piece of fish on the top half of the buttered foil and cover with a few slices of fennel. Scatter on dried chile, lemon zest, and a few bits of fennel tops. Place a bit of butter on the fish. Bring the foil over the fish and fold to seal each side, leaving the top open. Pour a little vermouth and lemon juice into each bag, then seal.

Place the bags on a baking sheet and into the preheated oven. Bake for 15 minutes, or until the bags inflate. Split open each bag and serve.

Sea bass baked in sea salt

Sea bass	1 (4½-lb)
Lemons	2
Coarse sea salt	6½ lbs
Rosemary sprigs	2
Ex. v. olive oil	

Ask your fish merchant to gut the fish and remove the gills, but not to scale it. Cut the lemons into wedges.

Preheat the oven to 400°F.

Place the salt in a large bowl and add 1 cup of water. Stir to stiffen the salt to damp sand consistency. Season the fish generously inside the cavity and add the rosemary.

Cover the bottom of a large, flat baking pan with a thick layer of salt. Place the fish on top, then pack the remaining salt over the fish, making sure you cover it evenly (see the photograph on the previous page).

Bake in the preheated oven for 15 to 20 minutes. To test for doneness, pierce through the salt with a skewer and into the fish to the backbone, where the fish is thickest. Touch the end of the skewer: if it is hot, the fish is cooked.

Remove the fish from the oven to cool slightly. Break off the now hard salt crust from the top. Lift the fish off the salt base, then remove the skin from the top side. Fillet the fish to serve.

Place the fish on a plate, and serve with lemon wedges and a very good olive oil.

Use a coarse-grained sea salt such as Costa, not Maldon salt, for this recipe.

Fish with . . .

Poached turbot, salsa verde

Salsa verde

Flat-leaf parsley leaves	2 tbsp
Mint leaves	1 tbsp
Ex. v. olive oil	
Garlic clove	1
Capers	1 tbsp
Anchovy fillets	3
Dijon mustard	1 tbsp
Red wine vinegar	1 tbsp
Garlic bulb	½
Fennel seeds	1 tbsp
Parsley stems	4
Black peppercorns	2 tbsp
White wine	1½ cups
Turbot tranches	4

For the salsa verde, chop the parsley and mint, put into a bowl, and cover with olive oil. Peel the garlic and chop with the capers and anchovies. Add to the herbs and mix. Stir in the mustard and vinegar, season, and add more olive oil to loosen the sauce.

Cut the garlic bulb in half crosswise. In a pan wide enough to hold the turbot pieces in one layer, combine the fennel seeds, garlic, parsley, peppercorns, and wine. Add 6 cups of water and boil for 30 minutes.

Reduce to a simmer and add the fish. The fish should be covered by the liquid—top up with hot water, if necessary. Poach for 10 minutes, then remove from the heat and drain.

Serve hot or at room temperature, with the salsa verde.

The flavor of the broth should be delicate and fresh. Choose a light, dry white wine such as Pinot Bianco.

Sea bass, potato, tomato

Waxy potatoes	1 lb
Cherry tomatoes	9 oz
Rosemary sprigs	4
Ex. v. olive oil	
Sea bass fillets	4
Anchovy fillets	8
White wine	2 cups

Preheat the oven to 400°F.

Peel the potatoes. Cut the tomatoes in half and squeeze out the seeds and juice. Wash the rosemary sprigs.

Cook the potatoes in boiling salted water until cooked but still firm, then drain and cool. Cut the potatoes into ¼-inch-thick slices.

Drizzle a baking pan with olive oil and cover with the potatoes and tomato halves. Place the rosemary on top; season. Place the bass fillets on top. Put two anchovies on each fillet with some black pepper. Drizzle with olive oil.

Bake in the preheated oven for 6 minutes. Add the wine, return to the oven, and bake for 6 minutes longer.

Serve each portion with juices from the pan spooned over.

Choose a thin-skinned, yellow, waxy variety of potato that will not break up when cooked a second time.

Fish with . . .

Langoustine, sea salt, olive oil

Parsley stems	8
Bay leaves	2
Lemons	4
Marjoram leaves	2 tbsp
Sea salt	
Black peppercorns	1 tbsp
Langoustines or crayfish	16
Ex. v. olive oil	

Wash the parsley stems and bay leaves. Cut the lemons in half. Wash the marjoram and shake dry.

Bring a large pan of water to a boil. Add the parsley, bay leaves, 1 tbsp sea salt, and the peppercorns, and return to a boil. Add the langoustines, pushing them down so they are submerged. Cover and cook until the langoustines are firm, 3 to 5 minutes, according to size. Drain.

Cover a plate with a thin layer of sea salt. Lay the langoustines on top. Drizzle with olive oil and sprinkle with marjoram. Serve with lemon.

We found this way of serving fresh, locally caught langoustines in Vernazza, a small village on the Ligurian coast. Perfect with just sea salt, fresh marjoram, and olive oil.

Grilled red mullet, crostini

Salted anchovies	4
Rosemary leaves	1 tbsp
Lemons	4
Small black olives	⅔ cup
Dried hot chile	1
Garlic cloves	2
Ex. v. olive oil	
Thyme leaves	2 tbsp
Red mullet	4 (1-lb)
Ciabatta loaf	1

Prepare the anchovies (see page 42), and finely chop. Wash the rosemary. Squeeze the juice from one lemon; cut the other lemons into quarters. Pit the olives, and crumble the chile. Peel the garlic.

Prepare the grill, or preheat the broiler.

Put the anchovies in a bowl and mix with the lemon juice. Finely chop the rosemary and add to the anchovies. Season with black pepper, add 2 tbsp olive oil, and mix well.

Pulse-chop the olives in a food processor. Put in a bowl and add the crumbled chile, the thyme leaves, and enough olive oil to make a rough paste.

Season the mullet on all sides, brush with olive oil, and grill for about 5 minutes on each side.

Cut the ciabatta into slices. Grill on both sides, then rub with garlic and drizzle with olive oil.

Put each mullet on a plate with the crostini. Spread half the crostini with anchovy and half with olives. Serve with lemon.

Fish with . . .

Raw tuna, bruschetta

Tuna	1 lb
Lemon	1
Dried hot chiles	2
Sourdough loaf	¼
Ex. v. olive oil	
Sea salt	

Slice the tuna across the grain into ¼-inch-thick slices. Halve the lemon, and crumble the chiles.

Cut the bread into four thick slices. Toast the bread on both sides. Drizzle with olive oil.

Serve the raw tuna beside the toast, sprinkled with chile, black pepper, and sea salt.
Serve with lemon.

Tuccino, a seaside fish restaurant just south of Bari, in Puglia, is where we ate a variety of raw fish. It was June when we were there, the season for bluefin tuna from the Mediterranean. The fish was incredibly fresh, the bread was made without salt, and lemon was the only accompaniment.

Fried scallop, borlotti

Dried borlotti beans	1¼ cups
Fresh hot red chiles	3
Garlic cloves	2
Ex. v. olive oil	
Arugula leaves	4 oz
Lemons	4
Sea scallops	16

Soak the borlotti beans overnight. Rinse, then put into a saucepan with one chile and the garlic cloves. Bring to a boil, skim, and simmer for 45 minutes. Drain, season, and add olive oil. Keep warm.

Slice the remaining three chiles diagonally into ¼-inch slices, leaving the seeds in. Wash and dry the arugula. Halve the lemons. For the dressing, squeeze the juice from one lemon and combine with three times its volume of olive oil. Season.

Heat a thick-bottomed skillet large enough to hold the scallops in one layer. Season the scallops on both sides. When the skillet is very hot, sear the scallops for 30 seconds on each side, then remove.

Reduce the heat. Add 1 tbsp olive oil to the skillet along with the sliced chiles. Squeeze the juice of one lemon over and shake the skillet for 1 minute.

Chop the arugula leaves and toss with the dressing. Add the borlotti beans and divide among four plates. Place the scallops, chile, and any sauce from the skillet on top. Serve with lemon.

Fish with . . .

Crab, chile, fennel

For 2

Garlic cloves	8
Fresh gingerroot	2½ oz
Fennel seeds	1 tbsp
Fresh hot red chiles	4
Fennel herb	¼ cup
Lemons	3
Tomatoes	4
Live crabs	2 (1¾-lb)
Ex. v. olive oil	¼ cup
White wine	1 cup

Peel and finely slice the garlic and gingerroot. Crush the fennel seeds. Wash and diagonally slice the chiles into rings, letting some of the seeds fall out. Wash and chop the fennel. Squeeze the juice from two lemons. Cut the remaining lemon into quarters. Peel the tomatoes, remove seeds, and roughly chop.

Cut each crab in half and half again. Use a hammer to roughly break the shell in the claws and thicker legs.

Heat the oil in a large, thick-bottomed pan with a well-fitting lid. Add the crab, garlic, gingerroot, fennel seeds, and chile. Stir briefly, then add the tomatoes, wine, and half the lemon juice. Season generously with salt and pepper, cover, and cook for 10 minutes.

Add the fennel and the remaining lemon juice. Serve the crab with the juices in a large bowl, with lemon quarters.

You have to buy small crabs, one per person, for this recipe. The difficult part is cutting them up live. Versions of this recipe can be found from China through India and into the Mediterranean.

8

Birds with wine

Roast grouse, Chianti Classico
Roast quail, Cabernet Sauvignon
Roast pheasant, Chardonnay
Roast partridge, Vin Santo
Pot-roast guinea fowl, Marsala
Roast wild duck, Nebbiolo
Roast wild duck, Pinot Bianco
Roast duck, Valpolicella
Roast chicken, Vermentino
Slow-roast chicken, vermouth
Roast chicken, Pinot Grigio

Roast grouse,
Chianti Classico

Plum tomatoes	8
Sourdough loaf	¼
Grouse	4
Sage leaves	2 tbsp
Thyme sprigs	8
Unsalted butter	14 tbsp
Chianti Classico	2 cups

Preheat the oven to 425°F.

Peel the tomatoes, leaving them whole (see page 66), then season them with sea salt. Cut the bread into four thick slices.

Stuff each bird with a few sage leaves, thyme sprigs, and 1 tbsp butter. Generously season inside and out.

Heat a baking pan and melt half the remaining butter. Add the grouse, breast-side down. Roast the birds in the preheated oven for 5 minutes, then turn them over. Add half the wine and the tomatoes, and roast for 15 minutes longer. Baste with the juices from the pan. Put the bread into the pan, soaking up some of the juices. Roast for a final 5 to 10 minutes, depending on how rare you like your birds.

Remove the grouse, tomatoes, and bruschetta from the pan. Add the remaining butter and wine to the pan juices and, over a high heat, reduce to a thickish sauce.

Serve each bird on a tomato bruschetta, with the wine sauce poured over.

Chianti Classico is produced in the heart of Tuscany. The ripe fruit, spicy character, and rich tannins of this wine are perfect for grouse, the gamiest of game birds.

Roast quail,
Cabernet Sauvignon

Organic quail	8
Garlic cloves	8
Dried hot chiles	2
Rosemary sprigs	4
Ex. v. olive oil	3 tbsp
Cabernet Sauvignon	1 cup
Can tomatoes	1 (14-oz)

Season the quail inside and out. Peel the garlic, keeping the cloves whole. Crumble the chiles. Wash the rosemary.

Heat the olive oil in a large, thick-bottomed pan. Brown the quail on all sides, then add the garlic cloves, the rosemary sprigs, and chile; fry together for 1 minute. Add half the wine and let it reduce, then add the tomatoes; season. Lower the heat and cook, half covered with the lid, for 10 minutes.

Add the remaining red wine and cook for 10 to 15 minutes longer. The quail should be almost falling apart and the sauce thick.

Serve two quail each with Wet Polenta (page 276).

Cabernet Sauvignon's subtle black currant flavor and big tannins combine well with the tomatoes in this recipe.

Roast pheasant, Chardonnay

Pheasants	2
Garlic cloves	4
Savoy cabbage	1
Unsalted butter	3½ tbsp
Ex. v. olive oil	2 tbsp
Pancetta slices	10
Sage leaves	3 tbsp
Chardonnay	1½ cups

Preheat the oven to 350°F.

Wipe the pheasants inside and out and trim off the fat. Peel the garlic cloves and cut in half lengthwise. Remove the tough outer leaves from the cabbage, cut in half, and cut out the core. Slice into ¾-inch-wide strips.

In a Dutch oven, heat the butter and 1 tbsp olive oil. Brown the birds well. Add the pancetta, half the garlic, and the sage. Cook to soften, then add the wine and bring to a boil. Roast in the preheated oven for 30 to 40 minutes, depending on size. Baste with the wine from time to time.

Cook the cabbage in boiling salted water until tender, about 8 minutes, then drain well.

Heat the remaining olive oil in a large saucepan, add the remaining garlic, and fry until soft. Add the cabbage, stir to combine, and season. Remove the pheasant from the casserole. Stir the cabbage into the wine juices and serve with the pheasant.

Chardonnay is our favorite white wine for roasting pheasant, bringing richness, floral aroma, and ripe tropical fruit flavors to the dish.

Roast partridge, Vin Santo

Quinces	2
Partridges	4
Pancetta slices	8
Unsalted butter	10 tbsp
Vin Santo	2 cups

Preheat the oven to 425°F.

Wipe the down from the quinces; cut in half and then in half again. Take out the core.

Season the birds inside and out. Place two slices pancetta over the breast of each bird and secure with string.

Heat a roasting pan and melt half the butter. Add the quince pieces and the birds, breast-side down, and brown briefly over high heat. Pour in half the Vin Santo and roast in the preheated oven for 10 minutes. Turn the birds and the quince over to brown on the other side. Add the remaining butter and Vin Santo and roast for 10 minutes longer.

Serve the birds and quince with the juices from the pan.

The season for partridge coincides with the quince season throughout most of Europe. If you have trouble finding quinces, you could use tart apples instead.

Vin Santo, Tuscany's famous sweet wine, adds wonderful apricot and orange flavors and a syrupy texture to the dish. Avoid the artificially fortified liquoroso versions.

Pot-roast guinea fowl, Marsala

Garlic cloves	4
Chicken bouillon cube	1
Guinea fowl	2
Prosciutto slices	8
Unsalted butter	5 tbsp
Ex. v. olive oil	2 tbsp
Sage leaves	2 tbsp
Marsala (dry)	2 cups
Heavy cream	1 cup

Peel the garlic. Dissolve the chicken bouillon cube in 1¾ cups of boiling water.

Season the guinea fowl inside and out. Lay four prosciutto slices over the breast of each bird and secure with string.

Heat the butter and olive oil in a medium-sized, thick-bottomed pan or Dutch oven and brown the guinea fowl on all sides. Add the garlic and sage, then cook for 40 to 50 minutes over a low heat, starting with the birds on one breast, then turning onto the other breast, and finally breast-side up. Add the Marsala and bouillon bit by bit during the cooking. There should never be more than ½ inch of liquid in the pan during cooking.

When the birds are cooked, remove them from the pan. Add the cream to the juices and reduce to thicken. Season.

Carve the birds, pouring the sauce over.

Marsala doesn't deteriorate after opening, so is a great standby in the kitchen. Like sherry, it can be dry or sweet.

Roast wild duck, Nebbiolo

Tomato sauce	½ cup
Prosciutto slices	6
Wild ducks	2
Nebbiolo	2 cups

Make the tomato sauce (see page 66). Tear the prosciutto into pieces.

Preheat the oven to 400°F.

Season the cavity of each bird. Mix the prosciutto with the tomato sauce, divide in half, and stuff each bird. Push the tail into the bird to seal the cavity.

Place the birds breast-side down in a roasting pan and pour in half the wine. Roast for 20 minutes. Turn the birds over, pour in the rest of the wine, and roast for 20 to 30 minutes longer. The breast will be medium cooked. The legs of wild ducks will always be tougher than domestic duck; longer cooking will give them a chance to become more tender, but the breast will then be well done.

Serve the birds with some of the tomato stuffing, which will have combined with the wine to make a thick sauce.

We use a basic Nebbiolo for cooking. The aged, more expensive, and grand examples of this wine, Barolo and Barbaresco, we reserve for drinking.

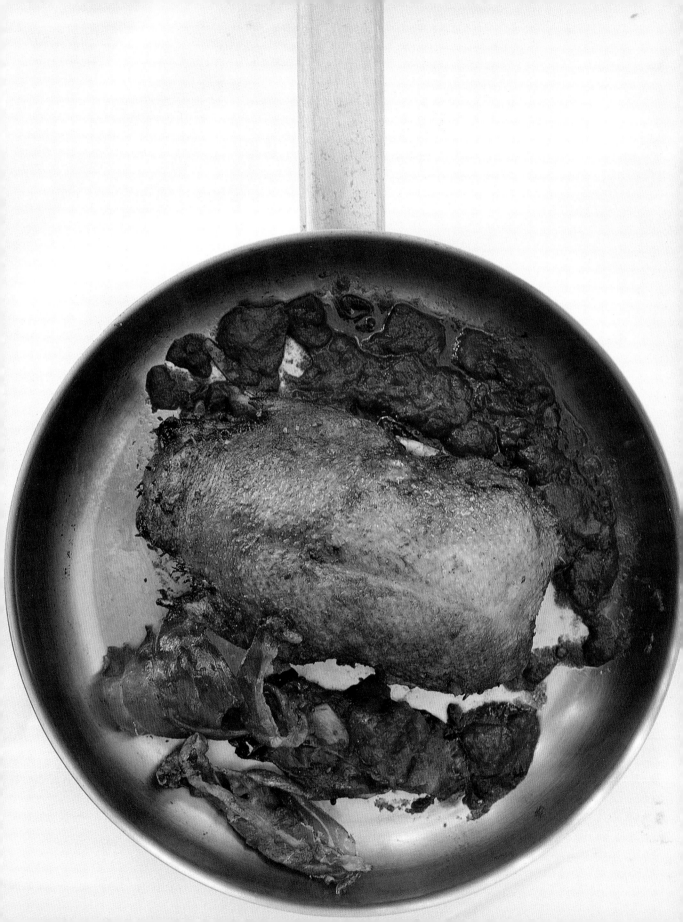

Roast wild duck, Pinot Bianco

Small wild ducks	4
Garlic cloves	4
Lemon	½
Ex. v. olive oil	4 tbsp
Thyme sprigs	6
Pinot Bianco	1½ cups
Arugula leaves	9 oz

Preheat the oven to 350°F.

Season the ducks inside and out. Peel the garlic and cut in half lengthwise. Squeeze the juice from the lemon.

In a Dutch oven large enough to hold the ducks, heat 2 tbsp of the olive oil and brown the ducks on all sides. Add the garlic and thyme and fry for a minute, then add the wine and seasoning. Bring to a boil. Roast in the preheated oven for about 30 minutes.

Remove from the oven and let the ducks rest for 10 minutes.

Combine the lemon juice and remaining olive oil; season. Pour this over the arugula leaves and toss.

Serve the ducks with the pan juices poured over, with the arugula leaves and borlotti beans (see page 277).

Pinot Bianco's lean, mineral character and floral aromas are excellent with the more delicate flavors of a tiny wild duck such as teal.

Roast duck, Valpolicella

Purple figs	16
Valpolicella	1½ cups
Large duck	1
Unsalted butter	14 tbsp

Place the figs in a bowl and pour in the wine, pushing the figs down so they are immersed. Cover and let marinate for 1 hour.

Preheat the oven to 350°F.

Remove the fat from the cavity of the duck and season the inside generously. Put 4 tbsp butter and eight of the figs inside the cavity. Smear the remaining butter over the breast.

Put the duck in a roasting pan, breast-side down, and roast for 45 minutes. Drain off the fat. Turn over, add the remaining figs and the wine, and roast for 1 hour longer, basting from time to time.

Skim off any excess fat and serve with the figs and juices from the pan.

Made from the Corvina grape, Valpolicella is meant to be enjoyed young. Its bitter cherry and almond flavors and refreshing acidity are a perfect balance to the fat-rich duck.

Roast chicken, Vermentino

Organic chicken	1 (4½-lb)
Waxy potatoes	2¼ lbs
Dried porcini	2½ oz
Garlic cloves	2
Rosemary sprig	1
Ex. v. olive oil	
Vermentino	1 cup

Ask the butcher to cut the chicken into eight pieces. Wipe the pieces clean with paper towels and trim off any fat.

Preheat the oven to 400°F.

Peel the potatoes and slice them in half lengthwise, then in half again. Soak the porcini in 1¾ cups of hot water for 10 minutes; drain, keeping the water, then rinse and roughly chop. Peel and finely slice the garlic. Wash and chop the rosemary.

Heat a medium-sized skillet with 1 tbsp olive oil, add the garlic, and lightly brown. Add the porcini, stir, and cook for 2 minutes. Add a little of the soaking liquid, stir, and gently simmer, adding more liquid to keep the mushrooms quite wet. Season.

Put the chicken pieces in a roasting pan in one layer. Add the potatoes, rosemary, wine, and 3 tbsp olive oil. Stir in the porcini and season. Roast for 30 minutes. Turn the chicken over and continue cooking for 30 minutes. The chicken and potatoes should be light brown. Serve with the juices from the pan.

Good Vermentino has a zippy, lemony acidity with peachy fruit and a hint of fresh herbs—great with potatoes and porcini.

Slow-roast chicken, vermouth

Organic chicken	1 (4½-lb)
Garlic cloves	3
Rosemary sprigs	2
Sage leaves	2 tbsp
Unsalted butter	10 tbsp
Extra-dry vermouth	½ cup

Preheat the oven to 200°F.

Wipe the chicken clean and trim off all the excess fat.

Season the cavity. Peel the garlic, and wash the rosemary and sage. Stuff into the chicken.

Place the chicken upside-down in a roasting pan just large enough to hold it. Add 1 cup of water. Roast for 1 hour, then turn onto the right side. Return to the oven and roast for another hour, then turn onto the other side and roast for yet another hour.

Remove the chicken from the oven. Raise the heat to 400°F. Rub the butter all over the skin, season well, and put the vermouth in the pan.

Return to the oven and roast for half an hour, or until brown. Drain off the fat and serve with the juices from the pan.

Vermouth, both red and white, is made from wine flavored with aromatic herb extracts and spices. We use extra-dry white vermouth for this recipe, which gives the chicken an herbal flavor.

Roast chicken, Pinot Grigio

Organic chicken	1 (4½-lb)
Garlic cloves	6
Rosemary sprigs	8
Lemon	1
Unsalted butter	1 cup
White wine	1 cup

Preheat the oven to 350°F.

Wipe the chicken clean and trim off excess fat. Peel and finely slice the garlic. Wash the rosemary and take the leaves off two sprigs. Halve the lemon.

Season the cavity and insert the garlic and rosemary leaves with half the butter. Tuck a sprig of rosemary under each wing and tie to secure. Rub the skin of the chicken with a lemon half and salt.

In a roasting pan, melt the rest of the butter. Place the chicken on its side with the rest of the rosemary underneath. Put into the oven and roast for 20 minutes. Turn the bird over and roast on the other side for 20 minutes longer. Then put it breast-side down and add half the wine and the other lemon half. Roast for a final 40 minutes.

Remove the chicken and rosemary from the pan, and skim off the excess fat. Over heat, add the remaining wine and cook for 5 minutes. Season, strain, and pour over the chicken.

The fresh, light, and appley character of this wine is a good complement to the strong flavor of rosemary.

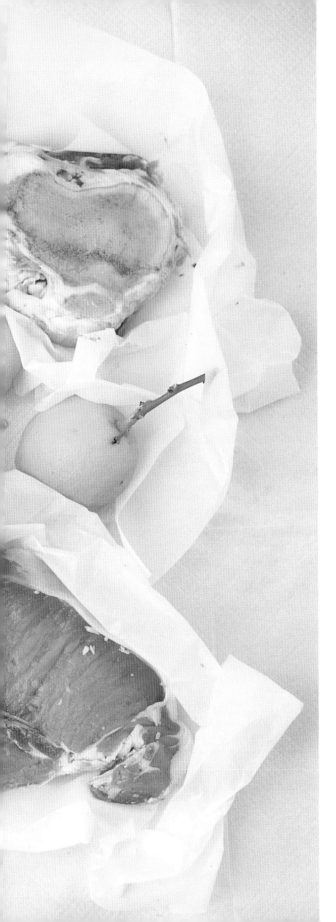

9

Roast meat

Whole leg of lamb, rosemary
Boned leg of lamb
Pork shoulder, slow-cooked
Pork loin on the bone
Thick veal chop, lemon zest
Veal shank, butter, white wine
Veal loin, tomato, capers
Cold roast veal, fresh tomato
Cold roast pork, mayonnaise
Beef tenderloin, red wine, horseradish
Twelve-hour beef shank

Whole leg of lamb, rosemary

Lemons	2
Garlic cloves	2
Leg of lamb	1
Small rosemary sprigs	2 tbsp
Ex. v. olive oil	

Preheat the oven to 400°F.

Peel the lemons, and cut the peel into small pieces. Squeeze the juice from the lemons. Peel and slice the garlic.

Cut small slits all over the leg, ½ inch deep, and stuff a little garlic, rosemary, and lemon peel inside each. Season well and rub with olive oil.

Place the lamb in a roasting pan and roast for 30 minutes. Remove from the oven and pour the lemon juice over. Reduce the heat to 300°F and roast for 1 hour longer, covered with foil.

Transfer to a board or serving plate and let rest for 10 to 15 minutes. Tilt the roasting pan to remove as much fat as possible, then pour the juices over the lamb.

Spring lamb is available from mid-April to December from lambs that are born the same year. The flavor of grass-fed lamb develops, getting stronger throughout the year.

Look for pale pink flesh with a very thin coating of white fat. The weight of the short leg we use is usually between 5½ and 6½ lbs and a full leg with sirloin between 6½ and 9 lbs.

Boned leg of lamb

Leg of lamb	1
Rosemary sprigs	3
Garlic cloves	6
Anchovy fillets	10
Lemons	2
Ex. v. olive oil	

Ask the butcher to remove just the long leg bone, keeping the butterflied meat attached to the shank bone.

Preheat the oven to 325°F.

Wash the rosemary and pull the leaves from the stems. Peel and crush the garlic, and chop the anchovies. Squeeze the juice from one lemon; cut the other in half.

Finely chop the rosemary with the garlic and 1 tbsp sea salt. Add a little of the lemon juice to make a paste and spread on the inside of the leg. Scatter on the anchovies. Roll the leg up into a sausage, tie with string, and season.

Place in a roasting pan and drizzle with olive oil and the rest of the lemon juice. Roast in the oven for 45 minutes with the lemon halves, then turn the meat over and squeeze the juice from the cooked lemons over the meat. Roast for 1¼ hours longer.

Remove the lamb from the pan to a serving platter and cut off the string. Add 3 tbsp of hot water to the pan, deglaze, and pour this juice over thick-cut slices.

Pork shoulder, slow-cooked

Pork shoulder	1 (4½-lb)
Garlic cloves	6
Lemon	1
Unsalted butter	10 tbsp
Ex. v. olive oil	2 tbsp
Sage leaves	2 tbsp
White wine	1 cup
Milk	1 cup

Ask your butcher to bone the piece of shoulder and remove any skin. (For four people, you would need a half small shoulder.)

Peel the garlic and cut each clove in half. Pare the peel from the lemon.

Season the piece of pork generously all over.

Heat half the butter with the olive oil in a medium-sized, thick-bottomed pan with a lid, just large enough to hold the pork. Brown the meat on all sides. Drain off excess fat, then add the remaining butter, the garlic, sage, and lemon peel. Fry to color the garlic, then add half the wine. Reduce the heat, half cover, and very gently simmer for 3 hours, adding more wine to keep a fraction of liquid in the pan at all times.

Start adding the milk after all the wine has evaporated. The milk should begin to curdle and thicken in the last half hour of cooking. The pork will be cooked when you can break it up with a spoon.

Choose your pork shoulder carefully—it should have a thick layer of fat. The fat renders down in the very slow cooking, keeping the meat moist and tender.

Pork loin on the bone

Pork loin	1 (3¼-lb)
Rosemary sprigs	2
Garlic cloves	4
Ex. v. olive oil	

Ask your butcher to cut the loin from the bone, keeping the rib bones intact, and to trim just the rib bones so that you have the bone and the meat in two separate pieces.

Preheat the oven to 350°F.

Wash the rosemary and pull the leaves from the stems. Peel the garlic. Chop the rosemary and garlic together with 1 tbsp sea salt. Rub the rosemary mixture all over the meat, then put it back on the bone in its original position. Tie with string to secure.

Place the loin in a roasting pan and drizzle with olive oil. Roast for 1½ to 2 hours, turning the meat over from time to time. Add 3 tbsp of water to loosen the juices during roasting.

Remove the string, cut the loin into thick slices, and serve with the concentrated juices from the roasting pan.

Pork is a popular meat in Tuscany. This recipe is known as Arista di Maiale and is the traditional Florentine way to roast pork loin on the bone.

Thick veal chop, lemon zest

Lemons	2
Veal loin chops, 1¼ inches thick	4
Ex. v. olive oil	
Thyme leaves	2 tbsp
Unsalted butter	10 tbsp

Preheat the oven to 400°F.

Wash the lemons and finely grate the zest. Season the chops and put in a bowl with 2 tbsp olive oil, the lemon zest, and thyme. Marinate for 20 minutes, then remove onto paper towels.

In a baking pan large enough to hold the chops in one layer, melt half the butter with 2 tbsp olive oil. Sear the chops over high heat to get a dark color. Remove the chops from the pan and discard the fat. Wipe the pan with paper towels.

Return the chops to the pan and divide the remaining butter over them. Season well. Put the pan into the preheated oven and roast for 15 minutes.

Squeeze the lemon juice over and serve.

Roasting a very thick chop, rather than grilling or broiling it, helps to keep the meat succulent and juicy. It is important to sear the chop first over high heat. Serve with salsa verde (see page 131).

Veal shank, butter, white wine

Veal shank	1
Garlic cloves	14
Unsalted butter	7 tbsp
Thyme sprigs	3–4
White wine	1 cup
Ciabatta slices	4
Ex. v. olive oil	

Preheat the oven to 400°F.

Season the meat generously. Peel the garlic.

In a thick-bottomed pan, heat the butter and brown the meat on all sides. Remove from the pan; discard the butter and put the meat back into the pan. Add 12 of the garlic cloves, the thyme, and half the wine. Cover with parchment paper and the lid, then put into the oven to cook for 15 minutes, basting occasionally.

Lower the oven to 325°F and cook for 2 hours longer, basting every 20 minutes. Add more wine so there is always about ¼ inch liquid in the bottom of the pan.

After 2 hours, remove the lid and cook for a final 15 minutes to brown.

Toast the bread on each side. Rub lightly with the remaining garlic and drizzle with olive oil.

The meat will fall into pieces off the bone. Tap out the marrow. Serve the meat with the juices and the crostini spread with the marrow.

Ask your butcher to cut the ends off the veal shank bones to reveal the marrow.

Veal loin, tomato, capers

Veal loin, bone in	1 (4½-lb)
Plum tomatoes	6
Flat-leaf parsley leaves	2 tbsp
Garlic cloves	4
Capers	3 tbsp
Unsalted butter	⅓ cup
Red wine vinegar	7 tbsp

Preheat the oven to 300°F.

Season the meat on all sides. Peel the tomatoes, remove the seeds, and roughly chop (see page 66). Chop the parsley. Peel the garlic cloves. Rinse the capers.

Melt the butter in a Dutch oven and brown the meat on all sides. Add the vinegar and let it reduce. Place in the preheated oven and roast for 1½ hours. Turn and baste the meat after the first half hour. After 1 hour, add the garlic and, 5 minutes later, the tomatoes and 1 tbsp sea salt. Continue to roast for 30 minutes longer, then add the capers and parsley and stir into the tomato sauce.

Carve the veal on the bone as thick chops and serve with the sauce spooned over.

The tradition of adding sweet, ripe tomatoes to the roast veal pan instead of wine to make the sauce comes from Campania, in southern Italy. Adding salted capers to the sauce was suggested to us by our Neapolitan friend Antonella.

Cold roast veal, fresh tomato

Tomato sauce	1 cup
Basil leaves	2 tbsp
Salted capers	⅓ cup
Cold roast veal	1 lb
Lemons	2
Ex. v. olive oil	

Make the tomato sauce (see page 67) and let it cool. Wash the basil, and rinse the capers.

Slice the veal as finely as possible. Squeeze the juice from one lemon and mix it with three times its volume of olive oil. Season. Quarter the other lemon.

Lay the veal slices over each plate. Season with sea salt and drizzle the dressing over. Spoon on the tomato sauce, and scatter the capers and basil leaves on top. Drizzle with olive oil and serve with lemon quarters.

This is the southern version of vitello tonnato, a summer dish that is refreshing as well as filling. The recipe comes from Puglia. Leftover cold pork would work just as well.

Cold roast pork, mayonnai

Cold roast pork	1 lb
Lemons	3
Capers	3 tbsp
Anchovy fillets	6
Parsley leaves	2 tbsp
Organic egg yolks	2
Ex. v. olive oil	

Finely slice the cold pork. Squeeze the juice from two lemons; cut the third lemon into quarters. Rinse the capers. Rinse the anchovies, then drizzle 1 tsp lemon juice over them and chop. Finely chop the parsley.

To make the mayonnaise, whisk the egg yolks with 1 tsp lemon juice, then add 1 cup olive oil drop by drop until you have a thick sauce. Stir in the capers, anchovies, and parsley. Taste for seasoning.

Mix the remaining lemon juice with three times its volume of olive oil, and season.

Lay the pork out on a large serving platter, season, and drizzle on the dressing. Spoon the mayonnaise over. Serve with lemon quarters.

This recipe is similar to Milanese vitello tonnato in that the pork is thinly sliced and covered with mayonnaise, flavored here with anchovies and capers rather than the traditional tuna.

Beef tenderloin, red wine, horseradish

Beef tenderloin	1 (3¼-lb)
Fresh horseradish	3½ oz
Crème fraîche	⅔ cup
Red wine vinegar	1 tbsp
Ex. v. olive oil	1 tbsp
Rosemary sprigs	2
Red wine	1½ cups
Unsalted butter	7 tbsp

Preheat the oven to 400°F.

Trim and season the beef tenderloin. Peel the horseradish and grate finely, then add the crème fraîche, red wine vinegar, and seasoning.

Heat the olive oil in a baking pan large enough to hold the tenderloin. Brown the meat well on all sides. Add the rosemary. Cover with parchment paper, place in the preheated oven, and roast for 15 minutes.

Remove the beef. Add the red wine to the pan and reduce by half over medium heat, scraping up the juices. Whisk in the butter.

Cut the beef into thick slices and spoon the sauce over. Serve with the horseradish.

When choosing beef tenderloin, look for outer flesh that is a bright purplish-red color laced with thin streaks of white fat. The meat should be firm to the touch and not at all wet. When cut into portions, the meat should have a fine texture and scarlet color.

Twelve-hour beef shank

For 6

Beef shank, bone in	1 (6½-lb)
Garlic cloves	50
Chianti Classico	3 cups
Thyme sprigs	8
Ground black pepper	3 tbsp
Sourdough loaf	½
Ex. v. olive oil	

Ask your butcher to cut a section across the shank, so that you have the sawn-off bone surrounded by meat as for osso buco, but here with beef. You will have one largish piece, which will be enough for six.

Preheat the oven to 200°F., or its lowest setting.

Peel the garlic cloves.

Place the beef in a Dutch oven. Cover with the wine and add the garlic, thyme, pepper, and a little salt. Slowly bring to a boil, then cover with parchment paper and put on the lid. Cook in the preheated oven for 12 hours. Take a look every 4 hours and replenish the wine if the beef is uncovered. You may need more than 3 cups (about one bottle). Test for seasoning.

Cut the bread into thick slices and toast on both sides. Serve chunks of meat on top with the garlic and the juices. Drizzle with olive oil.

This extreme recipe is based on the recipe for Peposo alla Fornacina, a dish from the area around the village of Panzano. Their flamboyant butcher, Dario Cecchini, who often serves plates of Peposo to his customers, introduced us to the dish, which was traditionally left to cook in the bread oven overnight.

10

Grilled
fish & meat

Flattened sardine, chile, lemon
Whole Dover sole
Whole side of salmon
Baby squid, marjoram
Halibut on the bone
Bass brushed with rosemary
Flattened quail, chile, salt
Lamb chop, bruschetta
Thick-cut sirloin, horseradish

Flattened sardine, chile, lemon

Sardines	16
Dried hot chiles	4
Lemons	5
Ex. v. olive oil	

To flatten the sardines, cut off the head and then prize open the fish. Press down to loosen the bone, then remove it from the flesh, pulling gently with your fingers.

Crumble the chiles. Finely grate the zest from three lemons; halve the remaining lemons.

Prepare the grill, or preheat the broiler or a ridged grill pan.

Rub the flesh of the sardines with chile, salt, pepper, and lemon zest. Place skin-side down on the grill and cook for 1 to 2 minutes. Turn over and grill flesh-side down for 1 to 2 minutes longer.

Drizzle with olive oil and serve with lemon.

This simple method of grilling boned and flattened small fish can also be applied to fresh anchovies, baby red mullet, and baby squid.

Whole Dover sole

Dover sole	4 (1-lb)	
Lemons	2	
Ex. v. olive oil		

Ask your fish merchant to skin the sole on both sides. Halve the lemons.

Prepare the grill, or preheat the broiler or a ridged grill pan.

Season the sole generously on both sides and brush lightly with olive oil. Place the fish on the very hot grill for 2 to 3 minutes, then turn over and grill the other side for 2 minutes longer, or until the fish is cooked.

Serve with lemon and a drizzle of olive oil.

The Dover sole season is from May to September/October, when the water starts to cool. Flatfish flesh changes, as the fish begin to roe at this time, the consequence being that the fish are thinner and softer, and not good to cook.

Whole side of salmon

For 8

**Wild salmon side
(whole fillet with skin)**   1

Ex. v. olive oil

Lemon   1

Season both sides of the salmon fillet and rub with olive oil. Quarter the lemon.

Prepare the grill, or preheat the broiler or a ridged grill pan.

Place the salmon skin-side down on the grill and cook for 4 minutes. Turn over and grill for 3 minutes longer. The salmon should be rare in the middle.

Transfer the fish to a platter skin-side up. Drizzle with olive oil and cut into thick slices. Serve with lemon.

This is a party dish. Grill over low coals. If you are cooking on a grill pan, cut the fillet to fit. It's important that the salmon is brushed with olive oil on both sides, to avoid the risk of sticking.

Salsa verde is delicious with all grilled fish (see page 131).

Baby squid, marjoram

Baby squid	1½ lbs
Lemons	2
Marjoram leaves	3 tbsp
Dried hot chiles	2
Ex. v. olive oil	

Clean the squid by pulling away the head and tentacles, along with the soft pulp inside the sac. Cut out the hard beak. Wash the tentacles and the sac, inside and out. Keep the skin and fins on. Pat dry with paper towels. Squeeze the juice from one lemon; cut the second lemon into quarters. Roughly chop the marjoram, and crumble the chiles.

Prepare the grill, or preheat the broiler or a ridged grill pan.

Season the squid generously, inside and out, and push 1 tsp of the marjoram inside each sac.

Mix the crumbled chile with 1 tsp lemon juice, 2 tbsp olive oil, and the remaining marjoram.

Place the squid bodies and tentacles on the hot grill and squeeze a little lemon juice over. Turn almost immediately—when the white flesh is lightly charred—and char the other side. Serve with the sauce and lemon.

The smaller the squid, the more tender they will be. For this recipe, choose squid with bodies no longer than about 3 inches.

Halibut on the bone

Halibut steaks	4
Ex. v. olive oil	
Lemons	2

Lightly season the halibut steaks on both sides and brush with olive oil. Cut the lemons into quarters.

Prepare the grill, or preheat the broiler or a ridged grill pan.

Place the halibut on the medium-hot grill and cook for 2 minutes, or until the fish comes away easily from the grill and is lightly browned. Turn the fish over and grill on the other side for 2 minutes.

Squeeze a little lemon juice over and serve with salsa verde (see page 131).

For this recipe, the halibut steaks need to be cut about 1 inch thick. Choose steaks with very white flesh, and be careful not to grill for too long, as they cook quickly and will become dry.

Bass brushed with rosemary

Sea bass	1 (6½-lb)
Rosemary branches	2
Ex. v. olive oil	
Lemons	2

Prepare the grill, or preheat the broiler.

Season the inside of the fish. Put one rosemary branch in the cavity and lightly rub oil over the fish, especially on the tail. Season. Halve the lemons.

Put 6 tbsp olive oil in a small bowl. Place the fish on the grill and brush the fish, using the second rosemary branch dipped in the oil. Turn over after 8 minutes, brush again, season, and cook for another 8 minutes.

Put the fish on a serving platter and serve with lemon.

The grill rack should always be very hot before starting to cook, to prevent the fish from sticking. Coat the fish with olive oil, paying special attention to the tail end. Rubbing with salt and pepper also helps.

Flattened quail, chile, salt

Dried hot chiles	4
Lemons	2
Organic quail	12
Sea salt	¼ cup
Thyme sprigs	24
Ex. v. olive oil	

Prepare the grill, or preheat the broiler or a ridged grill pan.

Crumble the chiles. Halve the lemons.

Dry the quail with paper towels and lay them breast-side down on a board. With poultry shears, cut out the backbone and discard. Press and flatten the birds.

Rub with sea salt and dried chile.

Place the quail on the grill breast-side down and scatter the thyme over. Grill for at least 5 minutes. Turn and cook for 5 minutes longer.

Serve with a drizzle of olive oil and the lemon.

Wild quail are larger and have much more flavor than farm-raised quail, but they are hard to find. If your quail are tiny, don't bother trying to flatten them—they will dry up on the grill.

Grilled fish & meat

Lamb chop, bruschetta

Lamb rib chops	16
Sourdough loaf	¼
Garlic clove	1
Lemons	2
Rosemary branch	1
Ex. v. olive oil	

Ask your butcher to trim fat and skin from the chop bones. Cut the bread into four thick slices. Peel the garlic. Cut the lemons into quarters.

Prepare the grill, or preheat the broiler or a ridged grill pan.

Season the chops on both sides. Place on the grill and brown on each side, about 3 minutes. Squeeze a little lemon juice over while grilling.

Grill the sourdough slices on both sides. Rub one side lightly with the garlic and with the rosemary, then drizzle with olive oil.

Serve the chops with the bruschetta, a piece of the rosemary, and some lemon.

This is great to cook on a grill, to be eaten with your fingers. Carefully trim all the fat from the chops, especially around the bone, as it will flame up and blacken on the grill, spoiling the flavor.

Thick-cut sirloin, horseradish

Boneless sirloin	**1 (2½-lb)**
Fresh horseradish	**3½ oz**
Red wine vinegar	**3 tbsp**
Ex. v. olive oil	

Cut the fat from the back of the sirloin, then cut it lengthwise into two steaks approximately 2½ inches thick. Peel the horseradish.

Prepare the grill, or preheat the broiler or a ridged grill pan.

Season the steaks on both sides, then place on the grill. Cook for 1 minute to sear them. Turn over and sear the other side. Continue to grill, turning the steaks to prevent burning, for 5 to 6 minutes longer for medium rare.

Slice the steaks as in the picture and serve with a small pile of horseradish finely grated at the last minute. Drizzle some vinegar over the horseradish, and some olive oil over the steak.

Fresh horseradish oxidizes quickly, which is why we suggest grating it at the very last minute.

11

Italian vegetables

Fried eggplant, basil, tomato
Roast eggplant, tomato
Roast whole pepper, capers
Zucchini scapece
Zucchini trifolati, tomato
Roast porcini caps and stems
Fried porcini, parsley, garlic
Smashed cannellini, olives
Green bean, potato
Half-mashed potato, parsley
Fennel, tomato
Roast celeriac, squash, fennel
Cavolo nero, fennel seed
Fava bean, pea, asparagus

Fried eggplant,
basil, tomato

Eggplants	2
Plum tomatoes	6
Garlic cloves	2
Basil leaves	3 tbsp
Ex. v. olive oil	
Sunflower oil	1 cup
Red wine vinegar	3 tbsp

Wash the eggplants and cut into slices ¼ inch thick. Lay them on paper towels and sprinkle with sea salt. Make a cut in the tomato skins, blanch in boiling salted water for 30 seconds, and remove to cold water. Peel off the skins. Cut each tomato in half and then in half again. Peel the garlic and slice in half. Wash the basil.

Heat 2 tbsp olive oil in a thick-bottomed saucepan. Add the garlic and brown lightly, then add 1 tbsp basil and the tomatoes. Season and cook for 15 minutes. The sauce should be thick.

Pat the salt off the eggplant. Heat half the sunflower oil in a large, flat skillet. When very hot, add a layer of eggplant slices. Fry briefly on each side to a light brown. Drain on paper towels. Continue frying, adding more oil to the pan if necessary.

To serve, lay the eggplant slices on a large plate. Sprinkle with the vinegar. Spoon the tomato sauce over the eggplant, but not to cover completely, then scatter the remaining basil leaves over the top.

Roast eggplant, tomato

Eggplants	2
Plum tomatoes	8
Parmesan	3½ oz
Basil leaves	2 tbsp
Ex. v. olive oil	

Wash the eggplants, then cut off the stem and the base. Slice into ¾-inch-thick disks. Place them in a colander and sprinkle with sea salt. Leave for ½ hour, then pat dry.

Preheat the oven to 400°F.

Cut the tomatoes in half, squeeze out the juice, and chop the flesh into small pieces. Grate the Parmesan. Tear the basil into pieces.

Place the tomato in a bowl, add seasoning, and toss with 1 tbsp olive oil, the Parmesan, and basil.

Brush an ovenproof dish with olive oil. Place the eggplant slices in the dish, brush with olive oil, and season. Bake in the preheated oven for 15 minutes. Turn over and spoon the tomato mixture on top. Return to the oven to bake for 5 minutes longer.

Of the many baked eggplant recipes in southern Italian cooking, this one differs in mixing the grated Parmesan and the chopped tomato. The eggplant is best eaten warm.

Roast whole pepper, capers

Red bell peppers	2
Yellow bell peppers	2
Ex. v. olive oil	
Marjoram leaves	3 tbsp
Salted capers	⅓ cup
Red wine vinegar	2 tbsp

Preheat the oven to 400°F.

Wash and dry the peppers. Brush with olive oil, place on a baking sheet, and roast in the preheated oven until beginning to blister. Turn over and continue to roast, about 30 minutes in all. Cool the peppers in a bowl, covered with plastic wrap to keep in the moisture. When cool enough to handle, peel the peppers and remove the seeds.

Wash, dry, and chop the marjoram. Rinse and chop the capers, and mix with the vinegar.

Lay the peppers out on a serving dish and season. Sprinkle with the vinegar and capers, scatter the marjoram over, and drizzle with olive oil.

In Puglia, they roast the peppers whole in a very hot oven, usually a wood-burning pizza oven, until the skins blister. This method softens and sweetens the peppers and makes them easy to peel.

Zucchini scapece

Zucchini	1½ lbs
Garlic cloves	2
Mint leaves	2 tbsp
Dried hot chiles	2
Sunflower oil	1 cup
Red wine vinegar	3 tbsp

Wash the zucchini. Cut them into ¼-inch-thick ovals, then cut each oval into thick matchsticks. Place in a colander, sprinkle with sea salt, and leave for ½ hour. Peel and slice the garlic as finely as possible. Wash the mint. Crumble the chiles.

Heat the oil in a high-sided pan to 375°F, or until a piece of zucchini browns immediately.

Pat the zucchini dry. Fry in the hot oil, in batches, until lightly brown. Drain on paper towels. Fry the mint for 2 seconds only. Drain. Put the zucchini in a dish with the vinegar, mint, and garlic sprinkled over. Season with salt, pepper, and dried chile.

This is a southern Italian recipe for frying zucchini. In Naples, the zucchini are cut into fine disks and deep-fried, then sprinkled with vinegar, mint, and raw garlic. In Puglia, the zucchini are cut into thick matchsticks— a good way to use up larger zucchini.

Zucchini trifolati, tomato

Zucchini	**1 lb**
Cherry tomatoes	**10 oz**
Garlic cloves	**2**
Basil leaves	**2 tbsp**
Ex. v. olive oil	

Wash the zucchini. Cut them in half lengthwise and then into rough pieces of about ¾ inch. Tear the tomatoes in half and squeeze out some of the seeds and juice. Peel the garlic and cut into slivers. Chop the basil.

Heat 2 tbsp olive oil in a skillet. Add the zucchini and garlic, and stir to combine. When the zucchini begins to brown, add the tomatoes, salt, and pepper. Stir well, then cook for 5 minutes.

Remove from the heat and add the basil. Drizzle with olive oil and cover. Let sit for at least 10 minutes before serving.

Vegetables trifolati is a method of slicing and cooking with garlic, olive oil, and parsley. Other ingredients, such as mint, wine, or chiles, are sometimes added. In this recipe we add fresh, ripe tomatoes.

Roast porcini caps and stems

Fresh porcini	**1¾ lbs**
Lemon	**1**
Ex. v. olive oil	

Preheat the oven to 425°F.

Cut the porcini caps from the stems. Carefully wipe the caps clean. Peel the stems and cut each in half lengthwise. Quarter the lemon.

Lay the caps and stems on a baking sheet and season generously with salt and pepper. Drizzle with olive oil and roast in the preheated oven until tender, about 10 minutes.

Serve with lemon.

Porcini mushrooms are called *cèpes* in France, *penny buns* in Britain, and *Boletus edulis* in reference books. They are the most prized mushrooms in Italian cooking. Their flavor is best when the porcini are fresh and firm. The season starts at the end of summer and ends with the first frost. Use large porcini for this recipe.

Fried porcini, parsley, garlic

Fresh porcini	**2¼ lbs**
Garlic cloves	**4**
Parsley leaves	**2 tbsp**
Ex. v. olive oil	

Clean the porcini carefully with a damp cloth. Separate the stems from the caps. Roughly chop the stems and slice the caps into ½-inch pieces. Peel and finely chop the garlic. Chop the parsley.

Heat a large, thick-bottomed skillet and add 2 tbsp olive oil, then the porcini. Shake the pan over high heat until the porcini begin to brown. Lower the heat, add the parsley and garlic, and continue to cook for at least 5 minutes. Season.

Drizzle with olive oil and serve.

The stems of porcini have an excellent flavor and texture. This recipe is great for using the smaller mushrooms and any broken pieces. Do not undercook porcini, as they gain flavor from cooking.

Smashed cannellini, olives

Dried cannellini beans	¾ cup
Baking soda	1 tbsp
Dried hot chiles	2
Young spinach	1 lb
Garlic cloves	2
Sage leaves	2 tbsp
Ex. v. olive oil	
Small black olives	⅔ cup

Soak the beans overnight in water with the baking soda. Drain and rinse.

Crumble the chiles. Wash the spinach and remove any tough stems. Peel the garlic.

Put the beans in a saucepan with the garlic and sage leaves, cover with water, and bring to a boil. Skim, then simmer for 30 minutes. Add 1 tbsp sea salt and cook until tender, about 45 minutes in total. Drain, keeping the garlic but discarding the sage. Add 3 tbsp olive oil, and roughly smash the beans and garlic. Season with half the chile and black pepper.

Cook the spinach in boiling salted water for 3 minutes, then drain. Press gently to remove excess moisture. While warm, season and mix in 1 tbsp olive oil.

Heat 2 tbsp olive oil in a small pan and add the olives, some black pepper, and a pinch of chile. Fry for 1 minute.

Put the spinach and cannellini beans on plates. Scatter the olives over the top and add a sprinkle of chile.

Try to find Taggiasca olives, which come from the Ligurian coast of Italy. Usually preserved in brine, they are deep purple and have a fruity flavor. They are similar to niçoise olives.

Green bean, potato

Fine green beans	**1 lb**
New potatoes	**1 lb**
Flat-leaf parsley leaves	**2 tbsp**
Garlic cloves	**2**
Ex. v. olive oil	

Trim the ends off the green beans. Scrub the skin off the potatoes. Finely chop the parsley. Peel the garlic and cut in half lengthwise.

Put the potatoes into a saucepan, cover with cold water, and add salt. Cook until tender. Drain. Cook the green beans and garlic in boiling salted water until tender. Drain.

Mash the potatoes coarsely with a fork. Mix in 2 tbsp olive oil and season. Smash the green beans and garlic with a fork, then add 1 tbsp olive oil and the parsley; season.

Combine the potatoes and beans roughly. Drizzle more olive oil over, and serve.

This is delicious in the summer, made with new potatoes and fresh green beans. It is really just a method of smashing them together with a fork and combining them with the olive oil. As the new potatoes are less floury, they remain firm and distinct.

Half-mashed potato, parsley

Waxy potatoes	1¾ lbs
Garlic cloves	2
Flat-leaf parsley leaves	5 tbsp
Ex. v. olive oil	

Peel the potatoes and cut each one into four pieces lengthwise. Peel the garlic. Chop the parsley finely.

Put the potatoes in a saucepan with the garlic, cover with cold water, and cook for 15 minutes, or until the potatoes are soft. Drain and season generously while hot.

Add ⅔ cup of the best-quality extra virgin olive oil and the chopped parsley. Stir in the pan, half breaking the potatoes into a mash.

This delicious recipe for simple mashed potatoes is designed to show off strong, peppery extra virgin olive oil. We had it first at the wine and olive oil estate Capezzana in Tuscany, where they prepared a November lunch around their newly pressed oil. Adding parsley cleverly deepens the greenness of the olive oil and gives texture to the mashed potatoes.

Fennel, tomato

Fennel bulbs	6
Garlic cloves	4
Dried hot chiles	2
Lemon	1
Ex. v. olive oil	
Can tomatoes	1 (14-oz)

Trim off the tough outer stems from the fennel, then cut each bulb in half and each half into sixths. Keep the green tops. Peel the garlic and slice in half lengthwise. Crumble the chiles. Squeeze the juice from the lemon.

Heat 2 tbsp olive oil in a medium-sized, thick-bottomed saucepan. Add the fennel and, after 2 to 3 minutes, add the garlic. Stir to coat with oil and prevent browning. Add the tomatoes, sea salt, and chile, stir, and cover with a lid. Turn the heat down to low and gently cook for 20 minutes, or until the fennel is soft and the tomatoes are absorbed into the fennel.

Chop the green fennel tops and add to the pan with the lemon juice and 1 tbsp olive oil.

The most tender Florence fennel is in the markets from December to March. The bulbs should be round, firm, and white, with feathery green shoots. Thinner green fennel bulbs will be tough and fibrous and are not suitable for this recipe.

Roast celeriac, squash, fennel

Celeriac	9 oz
Butternut squash	9 oz
Fennel bulbs	2
Garlic cloves	4
Plum tomatoes	7 oz
Ex. v. olive oil	7 tbsp

Preheat the oven to 400°F.

Peel the celeriac, then cut into ¾-inch pieces. Peel the squash, scrape out the seeds, and cut into ½-inch slices. Peel off the tough outer leaves from the fennel; cut each bulb in half and then each half into three wedges. Peel the garlic and cut in half. Cut the tomatoes in half.

Cook the celeriac and fennel in boiling salted water for 5 minutes. Drain and put into a large bowl. Add the squash, tomatoes, and garlic. Season generously and add the olive oil. Stir together to coat the vegetables evenly.

Place in a baking pan and roast in the preheated oven for half an hour. Turn the pieces over and continue to roast until all the vegetables are soft, up to 45 minutes in total.

Cavolo nero, fennel seed

Cavolo nero	2¼ lbs
Garlic cloves	3
Fennel seeds	1 tsp
Dried hot chiles	2
Ex. v. olive oil	

Strip the leaves of the cavolo off the center stem and wash. Peel the garlic; finely slice two of the garlic cloves. Crush the fennel seeds, and crumble the chiles.

Cook the cavolo in boiling salted water with the whole garlic clove until tender, about 5 minutes, then drain. Roughly chop it, including the garlic.

Heat 2 tbsp olive oil in a thick-bottomed saucepan and add the sliced garlic, chile, and fennel seeds. Fry until brown, about 2 minutes. Add the cavolo, season, and stir together briefly.

When buying cavolo nero, look for dark green leaves that are tightly crinkled and stiff. The correct flavor develops after the plants have had a few weeks of frost. If you cannot find cavolo nero, substitute kale.

Be sure to boil the cavolo until it is very tender. Drain gently, retaining some of the water in the leaves so that it is juicy rather than fried with the olive oil.

Fava bean, pea, asparagus

Fava beans in pod	1 lb
Peas in pod	1 lb
Asparagus	8 oz
Waxy potatoes	4 oz
Garlic cloves	2
Ex. v. olive oil	
Mint leaves	3 tbsp

Pod the fava beans and peas. Snap off the tough ends from the asparagus and cut the remainder into ½-inch pieces, including the tips. Peel the potatoes and cut into ½-inch cubes. Peel the garlic; leave whole.

Heat 3 tbsp olive oil in a thick-bottomed saucepan and add the garlic, potato, and fava beans. Stir together and cook for 5 minutes, then add the asparagus, peas, and 1 cup of hot water. Season. Simmer for 20 minutes, or until the liquid has been absorbed and the vegetables are cooked. Add more water, if necessary.

Chop the mint and stir in, adding a drizzle of olive oil.

Stewing spring vegetables together in olive oil is Roman in origin. There are many possible combinations—artichokes could replace the potatoes in this recipe, and scallions could replace the asparagus. All recipes include fresh mint, and extra virgin olive oil is drizzled over at the end.

Use frozen peas and lima beans if you need to save time.

Baked fruit

Blackberries, mascarpone
Black fig, almond
Apricot, molasses, ginger
Apple, orange, walnut
Plum, vanilla, bruschetta
Whole pear, cinnamon
Quince, brown sugar
Rhubarb, orange

Blackberries, mascarpone

Blackberries	2¼ lbs
Vanilla beans	2
Mascarpone	2 cups
Organic egg yolks	3
Confectioners' sugar	¼ cup

Preheat the oven to 400°F.

Wash and pick over the blackberries. Split the vanilla beans and scrape out the seeds.

Mix the mascarpone, egg yolks, vanilla seeds, and sugar together.

Put the blackberries in a small baking dish. Spoon the mascarpone over and bake in the preheated oven until the mascarpone begins to brown, about 5 minutes.

Mascarpone is a very rich triple-cream cheese from Lombardy in northern Italy. It is used for savory dishes as well as desserts. When heated, mascarpone melts into a creamy sauce. It keeps for at least a week in the refrigerator.

Black fig, almond

Blanched almonds	⅔ cup
Black figs	12
Lemon	1
Brown sugar	2 tbsp
Crème fraîche	⅔ cup

Preheat the oven to 300°F.

Split the almonds. Make a cross slash on the top of each fig, then squeeze from the bottom to open up. Butter a shallow baking dish large enough to hold the figs. Squeeze the juice from the lemon.

Place the figs in the baking dish and pour the lemon juice over. Sprinkle with the sugar and split almonds.

Bake in the preheated oven for 10 minutes. Spoon the juices over the figs and bake for 5 minutes longer.

Serve warm with crème fraîche.

Figs and almonds are a natural combination. Choose figs carefully—they should be soft but not squashed. Don't be tempted to eat figs out of season—they are best from June to September—or to buy under-ripe ones, as they lack the flavor of tree-ripened figs.

Apricot, molasses, ginger

Unsalted butter	3 tbsp
Apricots	1½ lbs
Fresh gingerroot	2 oz
Lemon	1
Molasses	5 tbsp
Crème fraîche	⅔ cup

Preheat the oven to 350°F., and use some of the butter to grease a flat, ovenproof dish.

Cut the apricots in half and remove the pits. Peel and finely slice the gingerroot. Squeeze the juice from the lemon.

Lay the apricots in the dish, cut-side up. Place a piece of the ginger on each apricot, with a small piece of butter and 1 tsp molasses. Sprinkle with lemon juice.

Place in the preheated oven and bake for 30 minutes.

Serve with crème fraîche.

Since Roman times, ginger has been used as a spice in southern Italian cooking, where it is often added to sauces, ice creams, and cakes. This combination of tangy ginger slices with sweet, ripe apricots and dark molasses is unusual, but it works well.

Apple, orange, walnut

Oranges	2
Granulated sugar	1 cup
Walnut halves	1 cup
Apples	4
Unsalted butter	3 tbsp
Crème fraîche	2/3 cup

Grate the zest from one orange and squeeze the juice. Cut up the second orange and pound in a mortar with a pestle. Push this through a strainer and keep the bitter pulp.

Put the sugar in a small saucepan with enough water just to cover. Gently melt the sugar into a syrup, then add the orange zest and pulp. Turn up the heat and boil to a caramel.

Wet a small oval dish with a spray of water. Put in the walnuts and pour the caramel over. Let cool and set hard. Unmold and crack the caramel into 1-inch pieces.

Preheat the oven to 325°F.

Core the apples and peel the top third. Stuff the caramel and a little butter into the core holes. Butter an ovenproof dish and put the apples in it. Scatter any spare caramel pieces around. Pour in the orange juice. Cover lightly with foil and bake in the preheated oven for 45 minutes.

Serve with crème fraîche.

It is important to use hard, green baking apples for this dish.

Plum, vanilla, bruschetta

Plums	1 lb
Vanilla beans	2
Granulated sugar	1 cup
Sourdough loaf	¼
Unsalted butter	7 tbsp
Lemon	1
Crème fraîche	⅔ cup

Preheat the oven to 350°F.

Cut the plums in half and remove the pits. Chop one vanilla bean and mix with the sugar. Split open the second vanilla bean. Cut the bread into four ½-inch-thick slices.

Thickly butter an ovenproof dish and put in the plums, cut-side up. Scatter half of the vanilla-sugar mix over. Bake in the preheated oven for 15 minutes.

Butter the bread and sprinkle with the remaining vanilla-sugar mix. Arrange in the baking dish, piling the half-cooked plums over the bread. Squeeze in the juice from the lemon; cut the lemon into quarters and add to the dish. Lay the split vanilla bean on top, then bake for 15 minutes longer. The bread should be slightly crisp at the edges, and soaked with the plums and their juices in the middle.

Serve with crème fraîche.

When buying vanilla beans, choose nice fat ones. Mixing chopped vanilla bean with the sugar makes the vanilla flavor more powerful in this dish. If you are a real vanilla fan, mix some of the seeds from the split bean into the butter for the bruschetta.

Whole pear, cinnamon

Pears	4
Unsalted butter	7 tbsp
Cinnamon sticks	2
Vanilla beans	2
Brown sugar	2 tbsp
Grappa	1 cup
Crème fraîche	⅔ cup

Preheat the oven to 300°F.

Wash the pears. Cut a small slice from the base of each one so that it will stand in the dish. Butter a baking dish that will hold the pears. Break the cinnamon sticks in half, and split the vanilla beans.

Rub some butter over each pear and place in the dish. Sprinkle with the sugar, vanilla, and cinnamon sticks. Cover the dish with foil.

Bake in the preheated oven for 20 minutes, then remove the foil and add the grappa. Return to the oven and bake for 20 minutes longer, or until the pears are very tender.

Serve warm, with the juices and crème fraîche.

Grappa is a strong spirit made from grape skins, seeds, and pulp after the juice has been pressed out for winemaking. It can be made from a single grape variety (e.g., grappa di merlot) or a blend of varieties. Use a white grappa, which will take on the pure flavor of the pears, not an oak-aged, golden one.

Quince, brown sugar

Quinces	2
Lemon	1
Unsalted butter	7 tbsp
Brown sugar	¾ cup
Crème fraîche	⅔ cup

Preheat the oven to 325°F.

Brush the down from the quinces, cut in half, and cut out the cores. Cut the lemon in half.

Thickly butter an ovenproof dish. Scatter the sugar over, reserving 4 tsp. Put a piece of butter and 1 tsp sugar in each core cavity and place the quinces in the dish, cut-side down. Squeeze a little lemon juice over. Bake in the preheated oven for 30 minutes, or until soft.

Serve with the juices and crème fraîche.

Choose ripe quinces that are yellow and firm, not soft ones, which are likely to be rotten in the center. Brush the down from the skin before baking. There are many varieties of quince; the smaller ones are most suitable for baking.

Rhubarb, orange

Champagne rhubarb	1 lb
Blood orange	1
Vanilla beans	2
Demerara sugar	3 tbsp
Crème fraîche	⅔ cup

Preheat the oven to 300°F.

Cut the rhubarb into 2-inch lengths. Finely grate the zest from half the orange, then squeeze the juice. Split the vanilla beans and scrape out some of the seeds.

Lay the rhubarb pieces flat in a small baking dish. Scatter the vanilla seeds, sugar, and orange zest over. Add the vanilla beans. Pour in the orange juice and bake in the preheated oven for 15 to 20 minutes.

Serve with crème fraîche.

Champagne rhubarb is the first bright pink rhubarb to appear in the markets around the end of January. It is a forced variety and is tender and sweet—you hardly need to do anything to it other than add brown sugar. We also add a little orange zest and juice—a classic combination.

If you cannot find Demerara sugar, substitute coarse light brown sugar.

13

Lemon desserts

Lemon, mascarpone tart
Lemon, ricotta, pine nut cake
Lemon, almond cake
Lemon semifreddo
Lemon, apple cake
Lemon, vodka martini granita

Lemon, mascarpone tart

Sweet pastry

Unsalted butter	¾ cup
All-purpose flour	1¾ cups
Salt	¼ tsp
Confectioners' sugar	½ cup
Organic egg yolks	2

Filling

Lemons	3
Organic eggs	4
Organic egg yolks	4
Granulated sugar	1 cup
Mascarpone	⅔ cup
Confectioners' sugar	1 tbsp

For the pastry, cut the cold butter into small pieces. In a food processor, pulse-chop the flour, salt, and butter to the texture of coarse bread crumbs. Add the confectioners' sugar and egg yolks, and pulse into a soft ball. Wrap in plastic wrap and chill for 1 hour.

Preheat the oven to 400°F.

Coarsely grate the pastry into a fluted 10-inch tart pan with a removable bottom, then press the pastry evenly to cover the sides and bottom. Line with parchment paper and fill with ceramic pie weights. Bake for 20 minutes. Let cool. Reduce the oven to 300°F.

For the filling, grate the zest from the lemons, squeeze out the juice, and mix together. Beat the eggs and yolks with the granulated sugar. Add the mascarpone and stir to combine, then stir in the lemon mixture.

Pour into the tart shell and bake for 1 hour, or until set. Let the tart cool, then sprinkle evenly with the confectioners' sugar.

Lemon, ricotta, pine nut cake

Lemons	3
White bread crumbs	1 cup
Ricotta	2½ cups
Granulated sugar	1 cup
Organic eggs	4
Organic egg yolks	2
Crème fraîche	scant 1 cup
Mascarpone	1½ cups
Lemon extract	1 tbsp
Pine nuts	⅓ cup

Preheat the oven to 300°F.

Butter the sides and bottom of a 10-inch springform pan.

Finely grate the zest from the lemons, squeeze out the juice, and mix together. Leave for 10 minutes to infuse. Make the bread crumbs (see page 277). Drain the ricotta.

Whisk the ricotta with the sugar until smooth. Add the eggs and egg yolks, one at a time, and continue beating. Add the crème fraîche. Finally, fold in the lemon mixture and mascarpone, and add the lemon extract.

Shake the bread crumbs in the pan to coat the sides and bottom evenly. Pour in the cake batter and scatter the pine nuts over the top. Bake in the preheated oven for 45 minutes, or until just set but still wobbly. Let cool, then unmold.

Pine nuts can rapidly become rancid due to their high oil content, so buy only small amounts and keep them in the refrigerator.

This is a Tuscan variation of the *Torta della Nonna*, a traditional cake made at Easter with raisins and pastry.

Lemon, almond cake

Lemons	4
Granulated sugar	1 cup
Organic egg yolks	5
Unsalted butter	10 tbsp
Blanched almonds	3 cups
Self-rising flour	⅔ cup
Organic egg whites	3
Baking powder	2 tsp

Preheat the oven to 325°F.

Use extra butter to grease an 8½ by 4½-inch loaf pan, then coat it with flour.

Finely grate the zest from the lemons and squeeze out the juice. Combine in a bowl and add the sugar and egg yolks. Put into a saucepan and cook gently, stirring, over a very low heat until thick. Stir in the softened butter. Strain through cheesecloth or a fine-mesh sieve and let cool.

Grind the almonds to a fine flour in a food processor. Add the almonds and flour to the lemon mixture.

Beat the egg whites to soft peaks. Sprinkle the baking powder over the egg whites and fold to combine. Fold the egg whites into the lemon and almond mixture.

Pour the batter into the prepared pan and bake in the preheated oven for 60 minutes. Let cool in the pan.

In most of the cake recipes using lemon juice, we also include the grated zest. Wash and dry the lemons thoroughly before grating. This is a simple cake, delicious for breakfast—a time when Italians eat their desserts!

Lemon semifreddo

Lemons	4
Organic eggs	4
Granulated sugar	1 cup
Heavy cream	1 cup
Fine salt	1 tsp

Grate the zest and squeeze the juice from the lemons; mix together. Separate the eggs.

Beat the egg yolks with the sugar in an electric mixer until light—at least 8 minutes. Place the mixture in a bowl over a large saucepan of simmering water (do not let the base of the bowl touch the water). Continue beating until the mixture comes to a boil. Let cool, then add the lemon mixture. Lightly whip the cream and fold in. Beat the egg whites with the salt until stiff. Fold into the lemon and egg yolk mixture.

Use parchment paper to line a pan that will fit into the freezer. Pour in the mixture and freeze until firm.

Semifreddo is half-frozen ice cream, with whipped cream folded into the mixture to give a mousselike texture.

Lemon, apple cake

Lemons	2
Apples	4
Blanched almonds	1 cup
Butter	½ cup
Vanilla bean	1
Granulated sugar	1½ cups
Organic eggs	2
Milk	⅔ cup
All-purpose flour	¼ cup
Baking powder	1½ tsp

Preheat the oven to 350°F.

Grease a 10-inch springform pan with extra butter.

Grate the zest from the lemons. Peel, core, and finely slice the apples. Grind the almonds to a fine flour in a food processor. Melt the butter. Split the vanilla bean and scrape out the seeds. Mix with the sugar.

Beat the vanilla sugar and the eggs together until thick and light. Slowly add the milk and melted butter. Fold the almond flour into the all-purpose flour, then stir into the batter. Add the baking powder, lemon zest, and three-quarters of the apple.

Pour the batter into the prepared pan. Put the remaining apple over the top and sprinkle with 1 tbsp extra sugar. Bake in the preheated oven for 1 hour.

Remove from the pan when cool.

Maria Manetti makes this delicious cake for us every time we visit the lovely Fattoria Fontodi in Panzano. Golden Delicious is the variety of apple she uses.

Lemon, vodka martini granita

Sugar syrup

Granulated sugar	¾ cup
Water	½ cup
Lemons	8
Ice cubes	8
Vodka	1¾ cups

To make the sugar syrup, heat the sugar gently with the water until dissolved, then boil briefly until you have a light syrup. Let cool.

Wash the lemons. Grate the zest from six of them and squeeze the juice from all eight. You should have about 2 cups. Mix the lemon juice with the zest and leave for 30 minutes.

Roughly smash the ice cubes. Mix the vodka with ½ cup of the sugar syrup and the lemon mixture, add the ice, and freeze in a tray until solid.

To serve, use a fork to scrape up the granita into martini glasses.

This vodka granita is a less alcoholic way of downing a martini. Serve it at the end of a special meal instead of brandy or grappa.

14

Chocolate & coffee

Bitter chocolate mousse cake
Hazelnut truffle cake
Coffee, walnut, hazelnut cake
Chocolate, vanilla truffles
Tiramisu
Panna cotta, chocolate
Chocolate, coffee sorbet
Rum, coffee truffle cake
Chocolate, almond cake

Bitter chocolate mousse cake

Cake

Unsalted butter	7 tbsp
Superfine sugar	½ cup
Organic eggs	2
All-purpose flour	1 cup
Baking powder	½ tsp

Chocolate mousse

Chocolate 70%	6 oz
Organic eggs	4
Superfine sugar	½ cup + 2 tbsp
Strong coffee	3 tbsp
Unsalted butter, softened	¾ cup

For serving

Brandy	⅓ cup
Heavy cream	⅔ cup
Unsweetened cocoa powder	1 tbsp

Preheat the oven to 350°F.

Use extra butter to grease an 8½ by 4½-inch loaf pan, then lightly flour it.

For the cake, cream the butter and sugar together until pale yellow. Add the eggs, one at a time. Fold in the flour and baking powder. Spoon into the pan and bake for 40 minutes.

For the mousse, break the chocolate into pieces, and separate the eggs. Beat the egg yolks with ½ cup of the sugar until pale, about 5 minutes.

Melt the chocolate with the coffee in a bowl set over hot water. Remove from the heat and stir in the butter, a little at a time. Add the egg mixture.

Beat the egg whites to soft peaks. Add the remaining sugar and beat until stiff. Fold into the chocolate. Cover. Chill for at least 2 hours.

Cut the cake into ¼-inch-thick slices. Line the bottom of the loaf pan with parchment paper and cover with slices of cake. Drizzle with half the brandy and spoon in a thin layer of mousse. Line the sides of the pan with cake slices, then fill with the remaining mousse and cover with cake. Drizzle with the remaining brandy. Cool for 1 hour before unmolding.

Whip the cream. Spread over the cake and top with cocoa powder.

Hazelnut truffle cake

Shelled hazelnuts	1½ cups
Unsalted butter	½ cup
Demerara sugar	6 tbsp
Chocolate 70%	9 oz
Dark rum	⅔ cup
Organic egg yolks	4
Heavy cream	1 cup

Preheat the oven to 400°F.

Using extra butter, grease the bottom of a 6½-inch springform pan. Line it with parchment paper and butter the paper.

Roast the hazelnuts for 10 minutes. Let cool. Pulse-chop in a food processor until finely ground.

Melt the butter in a small, thick-bottomed saucepan, add the sugar, and boil to lightly caramelize. Add the hazelnuts and stir until the nuts begin to stick together, 2 to 3 minutes. While warm, spread this mixture over the bottom of the pan.

Break the chocolate into pieces and melt with the rum in a bowl over simmering water. Cool.

Beat the egg yolks until pale. Stir into the chocolate, then slowly add the cream. The mixture will thicken immediately. Spoon into the pan and let set for 1 hour in the refrigerator.

To remove from the pan, soak a cloth in hot water and wrap it around the pan for 1 minute to slightly melt the edges. Unclip the side of the pan and carefully slide the cake off the base onto a cake plate.

This recipe comes from the restaurant Scacciapensieri, in Cecina, Tuscany.

Chocolate & coffee

Coffee, walnut, hazelnut cake

Instant coffee	5 tbsp
Shelled hazelnuts	1¾ cups
Vanilla beans	3
Unsalted butter	1⅔ cups
Granulated sugar	2 cups
Chopped walnuts	2 cups
Organic eggs	5
All-purpose flour	⅔ cup
Baking powder	1 tsp

Preheat the oven to 325°F. Using extra butter and flour, grease and flour a 10-inch cake pan, then line with parchment paper.

Dissolve the coffee in 2 tbsp of boiling water. Roast the hazelnuts in the preheated oven until brown, about 10 minutes. Let cool, then rub off the skins. Grind the hazelnuts to a fine powder. Finely chop the vanilla beans.

Beat the butter and sugar together until pale and light. Stir in the hazelnuts, walnuts, and vanilla. Beat the eggs into the mixture, one at a time. Fold in the flour and baking powder and, finally, stir in the coffee.

Spoon into the prepared pan and bake in the preheated oven for 1¼ hours. Let cool on a rack.

Using instant coffee in this recipe is intentional. The cake requires a very strong coffee flavor with as little liquid as possible, ruling out using filter or even espresso coffee.

Chocolate, vanilla truffles

Chocolate 70%	9 oz
Vanilla beans	2
Heavy cream	1 cup

Coating

Chocolate 70%	7 oz
Unsweetened cocoa powder 100%	½ cup

Chop the chocolate into small pieces. Put into a bowl. Split the vanilla beans.

Put the vanilla beans and cream into a saucepan and bring to a boil. Strain this over the chocolate. Whisk gently until the chocolate has melted, then let cool.

When the mixture is firm, set the bowl over simmering water just to warm it through. Remove from the heat and whisk well until smooth.

Put a sheet of parchment paper on a flat tray. Drop tablespoonfuls of the mixture onto the paper. Put in the refrigerator for an hour to set.

For the coating, melt the chocolate in a bowl over simmering water. Place the cocoa powder in a shallow dish.

Remove the truffles from the refrigerator. Dip them into the melted chocolate and remove with a fork. Transfer to the cocoa powder and roll around to coat. Refrigerate the truffles to harden for 15 minutes, then lift into a strainer to shake off excess cocoa. Return to the refrigerator to harden further.

Tiramisu

Instant coffee	½ cup
Brandy	1¼ cups
Savoiardi or ladyfingers	9 oz
Organic eggs	2
Mascarpone	2 cups
Confectioners' sugar	⅔ cup
Unsweetened cocoa powder	¼ cup

Mix the instant coffee with 1 cup of hot water. Mix the coffee with the brandy.

Lay the savoiardi or ladyfingers on a flat tray, and soak them in the coffee and brandy.

Separate the eggs. Mix the egg yolks into the mascarpone with the confectioners' sugar. Beat the egg whites to soft peaks, then fold into the mascarpone.

Using an oval, 14 by 10-inch ceramic dish, make a layer of wet savoiardi. Cover with a thick layer of mascarpone. Shake some cocoa powder over, then repeat with another layer of savoiardi and of mascarpone. Shake cocoa powder over and chill for a minimum of 2 hours before serving.

There are endless versions of this modern dessert. Ours is very rich and wet, with lots of alcohol and mascarpone.

Panna cotta, chocolate

Vanilla beans	2
Heavy cream	4 cups
Powdered unflavored gelatin	1¼ tsp
Milk	½ cup
Confectioners' sugar	1 cup

Chocolate sauce

Chocolate 70%	10 oz
Unsalted butter	3 tbsp

Split the vanilla beans. Heat 3 cups of the cream in a thick-bottomed pan. Add the vanilla, bring to a boil, and simmer to reduce by one-third. Remove the vanilla beans and scrape the seeds into the cream.

Soak the gelatin in the milk for 15 minutes. Remove the gelatin, then heat the milk until boiling. Return the gelatin to the milk and stir until dissolved. Add to the hot cream. Let cool.

Whip the remaining cream with the confectioners' sugar. Fold into the cooled cooked cream. Pour into four bowls and let set in the refrigerator for 2 hours or overnight.

Break up the chocolate and melt with the butter in a bowl set over simmering water.

Unmold the set creams onto plates, pour the chocolate sauce over, and serve immediately. This has to be done at the last minute or the chocolate will stiffen.

The panna cotta can be made the day before. The chocolate sauce can be kept warm in a double boiler. If you are feeling festive, pour a little grappa over the panna cotta before you pour the chocolate over!

Chocolate, coffee sorbet

Granulated sugar	1¼ cups
Strong coffee	⅔ cup
Unsweetened cocoa powder	1⅔ cups

Bring 2⅔ cups of water to a boil with the sugar and boil for 4 minutes. Let cool.

Add the coffee and cocoa powder, and cook over a low heat for 15 minutes, stirring to combine.

Strain. Churn in an ice-cream machine, or freeze in a shallow container, stirring every half hour or so.

This sorbet is very easy to make and inexpensive. Espresso coffee is our first choice, but you can also use a very strong filter coffee made with a higher ratio of coffee to water.

Rum, coffee truffle cake

Chocolate 70%	1 lb 2 oz
Heavy cream	2½ cups
Instant coffee	3 tbsp
Rum	7 fl oz
Unsweetened cocoa powder	3 tbsp

Break the chocolate into pieces, and melt in a bowl set over simmering water.

Warm the cream, then dissolve the coffee in it. Stir this into the warm chocolate with the rum.

Place a 6-inch cake or tart ring on a flat plate. Pour the mixture into the ring, and let set for 2 hours in the refrigerator.

To remove the ring, soak a dish cloth in very hot water and wrap it around the ring for 2 minutes. This will slightly melt the edges of the cake, making it easy to lift off the ring.

Shake the cocoa powder over the top.

We make this at The River Cafe for birthdays, as the recipe is easily adapted for any number. It is simply a flavored combination of melted bitter chocolate and cream.

chocolate, almo...

Chocolate 70%	6 oz
Unsalted butter	¾ cup
Blanched almonds	1⅓ cups
Vanilla bean	1
Organic eggs	2
Organic egg yolks	6
Superfine sugar	1 cup + 1½ tbsp
Unsweetened cocoa powder	⅔ cup
Organic egg whites	4
Salt	a pinch

Preheat the oven to 325°F.

Line a 9-inch cake pan with parchment paper, and grease with extra butter.

Break the chocolate into pieces. Cut the butter into pieces. Grind the almonds to a fine flour in a food processor. Finely chop the vanilla bean.

Melt the chocolate and butter together in a bowl set over simmering water. Let cool. Beat the whole eggs with the egg yolks and 1 cup of the sugar until light and airy. Fold in the cocoa powder and ground almonds. Mix together with the melted chocolate, then stir in the chopped vanilla.

Beat the egg whites to stiff peaks with the salt. Fold in the remaining 1½ tbsp sugar. Fold the whites gently into the chocolate mix.

Pour into the prepared pan and bake in the preheated oven for 35 minutes. Unmold when cool, and serve dusted with extra cocoa powder.

We use unsweetened cocoa powder from Valrhona to dust the cake. Put the cocoa into a fine strainer and sprinkle evenly over the surface of the cake. Do this just before serving.

How to make ...

Wet polenta

Parmesan	7 oz
Polenta flour	2 cups
Ex. v. olive oil	3 tbsp

Grate the Parmesan. Put the polenta flour into a large measuring cup.

In a thick-bottomed pan, bring 7 cups of water and 1 tsp salt to a boil. Reduce the heat to a simmer and slowly pour in the polenta flour in a steady stream, stirring with a whisk until completely blended.

As soon as it starts to bubble, reduce the heat to as low as possible and cook, stirring from time to time with a wooden spoon. Cooking will take about 45 minutes.

The polenta is cooked when it falls away from the sides of the pan.

Stir in either the olive oil or 10 tbsp butter and the grated Parmesan. Serve immediately.

Dried chickpeas

Dried chickpeas	1¼ cups
Baking soda	2 tsp
Celery heart	1
Garlic cloves	4
Potato	1
Dried hot chiles	2
Ex. v. olive oil	5 tbsp

Soak the chickpeas overnight in cold water with 1 tsp baking soda.

Remove the tough outer celery stalks; wash the heart and cut it in half. Peel the garlic and potato.

Drain the chickpeas, rinse well, and put into a pan with the remaining baking soda, the garlic, celery, and potato. Cover with water.

Bring to a boil, skimming off the foam that rises to the surface. Turn the heat down and simmer for half an hour. Add the chiles, 1 tbsp sea salt, and 3 tbsp olive oil. Continue simmering for 15 minutes longer, or until the chickpeas are tender. Let cool with the vegetables in their liquid.

To use, drain off most of the liquid, then mash the vegetables into the chickpeas. Check the seasoning and add the remaining 2 tbsp olive oil.

Dried borlotti & cannellini

Dried beans	1¼ cups
Baking soda	2 tsp
Garlic	1 bulb
Sage branches	2
Plum tomato	1

Soak the beans overnight in a generous amount of water with the baking soda. Cut the garlic bulb in half crosswise. Wash the sage and the tomato.

Drain the beans, rinse, and put into a thick-bottomed saucepan with the tomato, sage, and garlic. Cover with cold water. Bring to a boil and simmer, removing any scum that comes to the surface. Cook for approximately 45 minutes, or until the beans are very tender. Remove from the heat and let cool in the liquid. Season.

Bread crumbs

Ciabatta loaf	1

Preheat the oven to 350°F.

Cut the crust from the bread (stale bread is good). Tear the bread into small pieces and pulse-chop in the food processor to medium crumbs.

Line a baking pan with parchment paper and scatter in the bread crumbs. Bake for 10 minutes, or until lightly crisp. Store in airtight jars.

Dried porcini

Dried porcini	1½ oz
Garlic cloves	2
Unsalted butter	7 tbsp
Ex. v. olive oil	1 tbsp

Soak the porcini in 1 cup of boiling water for 10 minutes.

Peel and finely slice the garlic.

Drain the porcini, reserving the liquid.

Rinse the porcini under cold running water. Cut off any hard bits, then roughly chop. Strain the liquid through cheesecloth.

Melt the butter with the oil in a thick-bottomed skillet, add the garlic, and fry until soft, then add the porcini. Cook, stirring, for 5 minutes to combine the flavors, then add 4 tbsp of the porcini liquid. Simmer until it has been absorbed, then add the remainder of the liquid. Simmer until the liquid is reduced to a sauce and thick. Season.

Italian pantry

This is a basic list of pantry items that you will find useful when using the book. Included are items that can be kept for up to six months and also everyday fresh ingredients to stock up on once a week and keep in the refrigerator.

We suggest always keeping canned tomatoes and, for quick soups, good-quality canned cannellini and borlotti beans and various bouillon cubes (we use chicken, but vegetable bouillon cubes are fine). Essentials to keep in the bottom of the refrigerator are red onions, celery, garlic, and a few fresh herbs, such as flat-leaf parsley and basil in season.

Choose an olive oil for cooking, and an extra virgin, single-estate oil for bruschetta, soups, and drizzling.

Buy white sourdough bread with an open texture and crisp crust. In this book, we have used 2¼-lb loaves.

Pantry

sea salt
black peppercorns
dried hot red chiles
bay leaves (fresh or dried)
dried oregano
fennel seeds
nutmeg
bouillon cubes

capers
anchovies
black olives
extra virgin olive oil
red wine vinegar
aged balsamic vinegar
white wine
red wine
Dijon mustard

canned tomatoes
cannellini beans
borlotti beans
chickpeas
dried porcini
lentils (Le Puy or Casteluccio)

all-purpose flour
semolina flour
risotto rice
polenta flour
spaghetti
tagliatelle
short pasta

70% chocolate
blanched whole almonds

Refrigerator

unsalted butter
crème fraîche
Parmesan cheese
free-range organic eggs
pancetta

garlic
red onions
celery
flat-leaf parsley
sage
basil
thyme
marjoram

Suppliers

A.G. Ferrari Foods
Imported Italian delicacies
To find retail locations (in northern California only) or place a mail order:
877-878-2783
www.agferrari.com
Customer Service:
14234 Catalina Street
San Leandro, CA 94577

Agricultural Marketing Service (USDA)
To find a local farmer's market in your area:
www.ams.usda.gov/ farmersmarkets/map.htm

Arthur Avenue Specialties
Fresh mozzarella, pancetta, prosciutto, dried porcini, salted anchovies
Mail Order:
www.arthuravespecialties. com
Customer Service:
34 Winans Drive
Yonkers, NY 10701
914-923-8115

Browne Trading Company
Fresh fish, seafood, organic sea salt
Retail Market:
Merrill's Wharf
262 Commercial Street
Portland, ME 04101
207-775-7560, or
800-944-7848 [mail order]
www.browne-trading.com

ChefShop.com
Bottarga, salted anchovies, olive oil, baking chocolate, and other gourmet specialty products
Mail Order:
877-337-2491
www.chefshop.com
Customer Service:
P.O. Box 3488
Seattle, WA 98114-3488

Chocosphere
Gourmet chocolates from around the world, including Valrhona, El Rey, Amedei, and Green & Black's
Mail Order:
877-99-CHOCO [24626]
www.chocosphere.com
Customer Service:
P.O. Box 2237
Tualatin, OR 97062

D'Artagnan
Organic game and poultry
Mail Order:
800-327-8246
www.dartagnan.com
Customer Service:
280 Wilson Avenue
Newark, NJ 07105

D'Italia, Inc.
Italian gourmet food specialties
Mail Order:
888-260-2192
www.ditalia.com
Customer Service:
1401 South Boyle
St. Louis, MO 63110

Dean & Deluca
Specialty foods and premium wines
To locate retail locations or place a mail order:
www.dean-deluca.com
Customer Service:
2526 East 36th Street
North Circle
Wichita, KS 67219
877-826-9246

Diamond Organics
Organic produce, eggs, meat, pork, poultry, fish, and pantry items
Mail Order:
P.O. Box 2159
Freedom, CA 95019
888-ORGANIC [674-2642]
www.diamondorganics.com

Esperya
Bottarga, prosciutto, organic pecorino, olive oil, balsamic vinegar, pasta, rice, lentils
Mail Order:
877-907-2525
www.esperya.com
Customer Service:
1715 West Farms Road
Bronx, NY 10460

Formaggio Kitchen
Casteluccio lentils, imported dry pasta, organic specialty flours and polenta, olive oil, artisan cheeses
Retail Locations:
244 Huron Avenue
Cambridge, MA 02138
617-354-4750
and
268 Shawmut Avenue
Boston, MA 02118
617-350-6996
Mail Order:
888-212-3224
www.formaggiokitchen.com

Igourmet.com
Gourmet meats, cheeses, and specialty food items
Mail Order:
www.igourmet.com
Customer Service:
1735 Front Street
Yorktown Heights, NY 10598
877-446-8763

**Melissa's
World Variety Produce, Inc.**
Specialty produce available
in select retail locations
and via mail order
Customer Service:
P.O. Box 21127
Los Angeles, CA 90021
800-588-0151
www.melissas.com

Niman Ranch
Premium-quality,
hormone-free beef, pork,
and lamb available in select
retail locations
and via mail order
Customer Service:
1025 East 12th Street
Oakland, CA 94606
510-808-0340
www.nimanranch.com

Piccinini Brothers
Prime meat, poultry,
and game
Retail Shop:
Tartare
653 Ninth Avenue
New York, NY 10036
212-333-5300
Customer Service:
633 Ninth Avenue
New York, NY 10036
212-581-7731

**Royal Rose Direct /
European Vegetable
Specialties Farms, Inc.**
Cavolo nero, radicchio
Mail Order:
www.royalrosedirect.com
Customer Service:
1120 Growers Street
Salinas, CA 93901
831-758-1957

**Todaro Bros. Specialty
Food**
Imported olive oils, meats,
cheeses (including fresh
buffalo mozzarella),
confections, condiments
Retail Shop and
Customer Service:
555 Second Avenue
New York, NY 10016
212-532-0633, or
877-472-2767 [mail order]
www.todarobros.com

Zingerman's
Olive oil, vinegar, fresh
bread, cheese, and other
traditionally made foods
Mail Order:
620 Phoenix Drive
Ann Arbor, MI 48108
888-636-8162
www.zingermans.com

Index

anchovies
   anchovy, bruschetta, butter, 42
   boned leg of lamb, 168
   bucatini, sardine, salted anchovy, 80
   cold roast pork, mayonnaise, 181
   grilled red mullet, crostini, 136
   mozzarella, marinated
      anchovy, spinach, 15
   potato, capers, anchovy
      salad, 20
   sea bass, potato, tomato, 132
apples
   apple, orange, walnut, 237
   apricot, molasses, ginger, 236
   lemon, apple cake, 254
asparagus
   asparagus, arugula, Parmesan, 13
   asparagus, prosciutto soup, 102
   fava bean, pea, asparagus, 228
   linguine, clam, white asparagus, 92
   prosciutto, asparagus, 47

beef see also meat (salted, smoked
      & dried)
   beef tenderloin, red wine,
      horseradish, 182
   rigatoni, tomato, beef, red wine, 74
   thick-cut sirloin,
      horseradish, 202
   twelve-hour beef shank, 184
beets
   mozzarella, beets, tomato,
      capers, 10
blackberries, mascarpone, 232
borlotti beans
   borlotti bean, pappardelle
      soup, 108
   borlotti bean, sweet potato
      salad, 18
   finocchiona salami, borlotti, 56
   fried scallop, borlotti, 140
   rice, chestnut soup, 120
bottarga, mâche salad, 38
bread see also bruschetta; ciabatta;
      crostini; sourdough bread
   toasted bread, olives, vinegar,
      salad, 24
bresaola, Parmesan, balsamic, 54
broccoli
   broccoli, red wine soup, 122
   orecchiette, clam, broccoli, 89
bruschetta
   anchovy, butter, 42
   lamb chop, bruschetta, 200
   mozzarella, tomato, olives, 11

plum, vanilla, 238
   raw tuna, 138
bucatini, sardine, salted anchovy, 80
butternut squash,
   roast celeriac, squash, fennel, 224

cakes
   bitter chocolate mousse cake, 260
   chocolate, almond cake, 274
   coffee, walnut, hazelnut cake, 264
   hazelnut truffle cake, 262
   lemon, almond cake, 252
   lemon, apple cake, 254
   lemon, ricotta, pine nut cake, 250
   rum, coffee truffle cake, 273
cannellini beans
   mixed salami, two crostini, 52
   mozzarella, salami, cannellini,
      olives, 12
   smashed cannellini, olives, 218
capers
   cold roast pork, mayonnaise, 181
   mozzarella, beet, tomato,
      capers, 10
   potato, capers, anchovy salad, 20
   roast whole pepper, capers, 210
   Savoy cabbage, capers,
      parsley salad, 28
   smoked eel, celery, capers, 44
   spaghetti, raw tomato, arugula, 60
   veal loin, tomato, capers, 178
cavolo nero, fennel seed, 226
celeriac
   roast celeriac, squash, fennel, 224
celery
   chickpea, pork soup, 110
   mozzarella, celery, radish,
      Parmesan, 15
   smoked eel, celery, capers, 44
chestnut
   rice, chestnut soup, 120
chicken
   roast chicken, Pinot Grigio, 163
   roast chicken, Vermentino, 160
   slow-roast chicken, vermouth, 162
chickpeas
   chickpea, pork soup, 110
   tomato, chickpea, sage soup, 104
chicory, ricotta, prosciutto salad, 26
chile
   cavolo nero, fennel seed, 226
   crab, chile, fennel, 142
   flattened quail, chile, salt, 198
chocolate
   bitter chocolate mousse cake, 260
   chocolate, almond cake, 274
   chocolate, coffee sorbet, 272
   chocolate, vanilla truffles, 266
   hazelnut truffle cake, 262
   panna cotta, chocolate, 270

rum, coffee truffle cake, 273
   tiramisu, 268
ciabatta
   bread, tomato, basil, cucumber
      soup, 106
   grilled red mullet, crostini, 136
   mixed salami, two crostini, 52
   Savoy cabbage, ricotta crostini
      soup, 112
   toasted bread, olives, vinegar
      salad, 24
   veal shank, butter, white wine, 176
clam
   linguine, clam, white asparagus, 92
   orecchiette, clam, broccoli, 89
   taglierini, clam, fried zucchini, 84
coffee
   chocolate, coffee sorbet, 272
   coffee, walnut, hazelnut cake, 264
   rum, coffee truffle cake, 273
   tiramisu, 268
crab
   crab, chile, fennel, 142
   crab, fennel, tomato, radicchio
      salad, 34
   linguine, crab, 98
cream
   panna cotta, chocolate, 270
crostini
   mixed salami, two crostini, 52
   Savoy cabbage, ricotta crostini soup,
      112
cucumber
   bread, tomato, basil, cucumber
      soup, 106
   cucumber, mint, mascarpone
      salad, 32

ditaloni, mussels, white wine, 86
Dover sole, whole, 190
duck
   roast duck, Valpolicella, 158
   roast wild duck, Nebbiolo, 154
   roast wild duck, Pinot Bianco, 156

eel
   smoked eel, celery, capers, 44
   smoked eel, salicornia, 46
eggplant
   fried eggplant, basil, tomato, 206
   mozzarella, grilled eggplant,
      roasted tomato, 12
   roast eggplant, tomato, 208

fava beans
   fava bean, pea, asparagus, 228
   mozzarella, fava bean,
      olives, 11
fennel
   baked bass in the bag, fennel, 126

crab, fennel, tomato, radicchio
    salad, 34
fennel, tomato, 223
linguine, crab, 98
mozzarella, grilled fennel,
    prosciutto, 14
roast celeriac, squash, fennel, 224
fennel seeds
    cavolo nero, fennel seed, 226
    crab, chile, fennel, 142
    linguine, crab, 98
    poached turbot, salsa verde, 131
figs
    black fig, almond, 234
    roast duck, Valpolicella, 158
fish
    baby squid, marjoram, 193
    baked bass in the bag, fennel, 126
    bass brushed with rosemary, 196
    bucatini, sardine, salted anchovy, 80
    crab, chile, fennel, 142
    ditaloni, mussels, white wine, 86
    flattened sardine,
        chile, lemon, 188
    fried scallop, borlotti, 140
    grilled red mullet, crostini, 136
    halibut on the bone, 194
    langoustine, sea salt, olive oil, 134
    linguine, clam, white asparagus, 92
    linguine, crab, 98
    linguine, sardine, saffron, 78
    orecchiette, clam, broccoli, 89
    orecchiette, scallop, arugula, 81
    poached turbot, salsa verde, 131
    raw tuna, bruschetta, 138
    sea bass baked in sea salt, 130
    sea bass, potato, tomato, 132
    spaghetti, roasted red mullet, 94
    spaghetti, squid, zucchini, 82
    tagliatelle, langoustine, ricotta, 88
    tagliatelle, shrimp, pea, 90
    tagliatelle, zucchini, mullet, 96
    taglierini, clam, fried zucchini, 84
    whole Dover sole, 190
    whole side of salmon, 192
fish (salted, smoked & dried)
    anchovy, bruschetta, butter, 42
    bottarga, mâche salad, 38
    smoked eel, celery, capers, 44
    smoked eel, salicornia, 46
    smoked haddock carpaccio, 40
fruit (baked) see also individual fruits
    apple, orange, walnut, 237
    apricot, molasses, ginger, 236
    black fig, almond, 234
    blackberries, mascarpone, 232
    plum, vanilla, bruschetta, 238
    quince, brown sugar, 242
    rhubarb, orange, 244
    whole pear, cinnamon, 240

garlic
    fennel, tomato, 223
    fried porcini, parsley, garlic, 217
    twelve-hour beef shank, 184
Gorgonzola
    radicchio, walnut, Gorgonzola
        salad, 22
granita
    lemon vodka martini granita, 256
grappa
    whole pear, cinnamon, 240
green beans
    green bean, mustard salad, 31
    green bean, Parmesan salad, 30
    green bean, potato, 220
    potato, green bean, tomato salad, 21
    spaghetti, tomato, green bean, 70
grilling
    baby squid, marjoram, 193
    bass brushed with rosemary, 196
    flattened quail, chile, salt, 198
    flattened sardine,
        chile, lemon, 188
    halibut on the bone, 194
    lamb chop, bruschetta, 200
    thick-cut sirloin,
        horseradish, 202
    whole Dover sole, 190
    whole side of salmon, 192
grouse
    roast grouse, Chianti Classico, 146
guinea fowl
    pot-roast guinea fowl, Marsala, 153

haddock
    smoked haddock carpaccio, 40
halibut
    halibut on the bone, 194
hazelnuts
    coffee, walnut, hazelnut cake, 264
    hazelnut truffle cake, 262
horseradish
    beef tenderloin, red wine,
        horseradish, 182
    smoked eel, salicornia, 46
    thick-cut sirloin, horseradish, 202

ice cream
    lemon semifreddo, 253

lamb
    boned leg of lamb, 168
    lamb chop, bruschetta, 200
    whole leg of lamb, rosemary, 166
langoustines
    langoustine, sea salt, olive oil, 134
    tagliatelle, langoustine, ricotta, 88
lemon
    lemon, almond cake, 252
    lemon, apple cake, 254

lemon, mascarpone tart, 248
lemon, ricotta, pine nut cake, 250
lemon semifreddo, 253
lemon, vodka martini
    granita, 256
linguine
    linguine, clam, white asparagus, 92
    linguine, crab, 98
    linguine, sardine, saffron, 78

mâche
    bottarga, mâche salad, 38
mascarpone
    blackberries, mascarpone, 232
    cucumber, mint, mascarpone
        salad, 32
    lemon, mascarpone tart, 248
    pumpkin, mascarpone soup, 118
    tiramisu, 268
mayonnaise
    cold roast pork, mayonnaise, 181
meat (salted, smoked & dried)
    bresaola, Parmesan, balsamic, 54
    finocchiona salami, borlotti, 56
    mixed salami, two crostini, 52
    pappardelle, tomato, pancetta, 72
    prosciutto, arugula, 50
    prosciutto, asparagus, 47
    prosciutto, melon, 48
melon
    prosciutto, melon, 48
mozzarella
    asparagus, arugula, Parmesan, 13
    beet, tomato, capers, 10
    bruschetta, tomato, olives, 11
    celery, radish, Parmesan, 15
    fava bean, olives, 11
    grilled eggplant, roasted tomato, 12
    grilled fennel, prosciutto, 14
    marinated anchovy, spinach, 15
    raw zucchini, prosciutto, 14
    salami, cannellini, olives, 12
    summer herb, crème fraîche, 13
mushrooms see also porcini
        mushrooms
    mushroom, barley soup, 116
mussels
    ditaloni, mussels, white wine, 86

olives
    grilled red mullet, crostini, 136
    mixed salami, two crostini, 52
    mozzarella, bruschetta,
        tomato, olives, 11
    mozzarella, fava bean,
        olives, 11
    mozzarella, salami, cannellini,
        olives, 12
    smashed cannellini, olives, 218
    spaghetti, roasted red mullet, 94

toasted bread, olives, vinegar
	salad, 24
oranges
	apple, orange, walnut, 237
	rhubarb, orange, 244
orecchiette
	orecchiette, clam, broccoli, 89
	orecchiette, scallop, arugula, 81
	orecchiette, tomato, ricotta, 68

pancetta
	borlotti bean, pappardelle soup, 108
	pappardelle, tomato, pancetta, 72
	rice, chestnut soup, 120
	roast partridge, Vin Santo, 152
	roast pheasant, Chardonnay, 150
panna cotta, chocolate, 270
pappardelle
	borlotti bean, pappardelle soup, 108
	pappardelle, tomato, pancetta, 72
Parmesan
	asparagus, arugula, Parmesan, 13
	bresaola, Parmesan, balsamic, 54
	green bean, Parmesan salad, 30
	mozzarella, celery, radish,
		Parmesan, 15
	roast eggplant, tomato, 208
parsley
	fried porcini, parsley, garlic, 217
	green bean, potato, 220
	half-mashed potato, parsley, 222
	Savoy cabbage, capers,
		parsley salad, 28
partridge
	roast partridge, Vin Santo, 152
pasta
	borlotti bean, pappardelle soup, 108
	tomato, chickpea, sage soup, 104
pasta (fish)
	bucatini, sardine, salted anchovy, 80
	ditaloni, mussels, white wine, 86
	linguine, clam, white asparagus, 92
	linguine, crab, 98
	linguine, sardine, saffron, 78
	orecchiette, clam, broccoli, 89
	orecchiette, scallop, arugula, 81
	spaghetti, roasted red mullet, 94
	spaghetti, squid, zucchini, 82
	tagliatelle, langoustine, ricotta, 88
	tagliatelle, shrimp, pea, 90
	tagliatelle, zucchini, mullet, 96
	taglierini, clam, fried zucchini, 84
pasta (tomato)
	orecchiette, tomato, ricotta, 68
	pappardelle, tomato, pancetta, 72
	penne, tomato, dried porcini, 64
	rigatoni, tomato, beef, red wine, 74
	spaghetti, boiled tomato, 66
	spaghetti, boiled tomato two, 67
	spaghetti, raw tomato, arugula, 60

spaghetti, tomato, green bean, 70
tagliatelle, tomato, basil, 62
tomato, chickpea, sage soup, 104
pears
	whole pear, cinnamon, 240
peas
	fava bean, pea, asparagus, 228
	pea, zucchini soup, 114
	tagliatelle, shrimp, pea, 90
penne, tomato, dried porcini, 64
peppers
	roast whole pepper, capers, 210
pheasant
	roast pheasant, Chardonnay, 150
plum, vanilla, bruschetta, 238
porcini mushrooms see also
		mushrooms
	fried porcini, parsley, garlic, 217
	mushroom, barley soup, 116
	penne, tomato, dried porcini, 64
	roast chicken, Vermentino, 160
	roast porcini caps and stems, 216
pork
	chickpea, pork soup, 110
	cold roast pork, mayonnaise, 181
	pork loin on the bone, 174
	pork shoulder, slow-cooked, 170
potatoes
	asparagus, prosciutto soup, 102
	borlotti bean, pappardelle
		soup, 108
	chickpea, pork soup, 110
	fava bean, pea, asparagus, 228
	green bean, potato, 220
	half-mashed potato, parsley, 222
	mushroom, barley soup, 116
	potato, capers, anchovy salad, 20
	potato, green bean, tomato salad, 21
	pumpkin, mascarpone soup, 118
	roast chicken, Vermentino, 160
	sea bass, potato, tomato, 132
prosciutto
	asparagus, prosciutto soup, 102
	chicory, ricotta,
		prosciutto salad, 26
	mozzarella, grilled fennel,
		prosciutto, 14
	mozzarella, raw zucchini,
		prosciutto, 10
	pot-roast guinea fowl, Marsala, 153
	prosciutto, arugula, 50
	prosciutto, asparagus, 47
	prosciutto, melon, 48
	roast wild duck, Nebbiolo, 154
pumpkin
	pumpkin, mascarpone soup, 118
	roast celeriac, squash, fennel, 224
quail
	flattened quail, chile, salt, 198
	roast quail, Cabernet Sauvignon, 148

quince
	quince, brown sugar, 242
	roast partridge, Vin Santo, 152

radicchio
	crab, fennel, tomato, radicchio
		salad, 34
	radicchio, walnut, Gorgonzola
		salad, 22
radish
	mozzarella, celery, radish,
		Parmesan, 15
red mullet
	grilled red mullet, crostini, 136
	spaghetti, roasted red mullet, 94
	tagliatelle, zucchini, mullet, 96
rhubarb, orange, 244
rice, chestnut soup, 120
ricotta
	chicory, ricotta, prosciutto salad, 26
	lemon, ricotta, pine nut cake, 250
	orecchiette, tomato, ricotta, 68
	Savoy cabbage, ricotta
		crostini soup, 112
	tagliatelle, langoustine, ricotta, 88
rigatoni, tomato, beef, red wine, 74
rum, coffee truffle cake, 273

salads
	borlotti bean, sweet potato, 18
	bottarga, mâche, 38
	chicory, ricotta, prosciutto, 26
	crab, fennel, tomato, radicchio, 34
	cucumber, mint, mascarpone, 32
	green bean, mustard, 31
	green bean, Parmesan, 30
	potato, capers, anchovy, 20
	potato, green bean, tomato, 21
	radicchio, walnut, Gorgonzola, 22
	Savoy cabbage, capers, parsley, 28
	toasted bread, olives, vinegar, 24
salami
	Finocchiona salami, borlotti, 56
	mixed salami, two crostini, 52
	mozzarella, salami, cannellini,
		olives, 12
salicornia
	smoked eel, salicornia, 46
salmon
	whole side of salmon, 192
salsa verde
	poached turbot, salsa verde, 131
sardines
	bucatini, sardine, salted anchovy, 80
	flattened sardine,
		chile, lemon, 188
	linguine, sardine, saffron, 78
Savoy cabbage
	roast pheasant, Chardonnay, 150
	Savoy cabbage, capers,

parsley salad, 28
Savoy cabbage, ricotta
   crostini soup, 112
scallops
   fried scallop, borlotti, 140
   orecchiette, scallop, arugula, 81
sea bass
   baked bass in the bag, fennel, 126
   bass brushed with rosemary, 196
   sea bass baked in sea salt, 130
   sea bass, potato, tomato, 132
shrimp
   tagliatelle, shrimp, pea, 90
sorbet
   chocolate, coffee sorbet, 272
soups
   asparagus, prosciutto, 102
   borlotti bean, pappardelle, 108
   bread, tomato, basil, cucumber, 106
   broccoli, red wine, 122
   chickpea, pork, 110
   mushroom, barley, 116
   pea, zucchini, 114
   pumpkin, mascarpone, 118
   rice, chestnut, 120
   Savoy cabbage, ricotta crostini, 112
   tomato, chickpea, sage, 104
sourdough bread
   lamb chop, bruschetta, 200
   plum, vanilla, bruschetta, 238
   raw tuna, bruschetta 138
   roast grouse, Chianti Classico, 146
spaghetti
   spaghetti, boiled tomato, 66
   spaghetti, boiled tomato two, 67
   spaghetti, raw tomato, arugula, 60
   spaghetti, roasted red mullet, 94
   spaghetti, squid, zucchini, 82
   spaghetti, tomato, green bean, 70
spinach
   asparagus, prosciutto soup, 102
   chicory, ricotta, prosciutto salad, 26
   mozzarella, marinated anchovy,
      spinach, 15
   smashed cannellini, olives, 218
squid
   baby squid, marjoram, 193
   spaghetti, squid, zucchini, 82
sweet potato
   borlotti bean, sweet potato salad, 18
Swiss chard,
   mozzarella, summer herb,
      crème fraîche, 13

tagliatelle
   tagliatelle, langoustine, ricotta, 88
   tagliatelle, shrimp, pea, 90
   tagliatelle, tomato, basil, 62
   tagliatelle, zucchini, mullet, 96
taglierini, clam, fried zucchini, 84

tiramisu, 268
tomatoes
   bottarga, mâche salad, 38
   bread, tomato, basil,
      cucumber soup, 106
   bucatini, sardine, salted anchovy, 80
   cold roast veal, fresh tomato, 180
   crab, chile, fennel, 142
   crab, fennel, tomato, radicchio
      salad, 34
   fennel, tomato, 223
   finocchiona salami, borlotti, 56
   fried eggplant, basil, tomato, 206
   mozzarella, beet, tomato,
      capers, 10
   mozzarella, bruschetta, tomato,
      olives, 11
   mozzarella, grilled eggplant,
      roasted tomato, 12
   mushroom, barley soup, 116
   orecchiette, tomato, ricotta, 68
   pappardelle, tomato, pancetta, 72
   penne, tomato, dried porcini, 64
   roast quail,
      Cabernet Sauvignon, 148
   potato, green bean, tomato salad, 21
   pumpkin, mascarpone soup, 118
   rigatoni, tomato, beef, red wine, 74
   roast celeriac, squash, fennel, 224
   roast eggplant, tomato, 208
   roast grouse, Chianti Classico, 146
   sea bass, potato, tomato, 132
   spaghetti, boiled tomato, 66
   spaghetti, boiled tomato two, 67
   spaghetti, raw tomato, arugula, 60
   spaghetti, roasted red mullet, 94
   spaghetti, tomato, green bean, 70
   tagliatelle, tomato, basil, 62
   tagliatelle, zucchini, mullet, 96
   tomato, chickpea, sage soup, 104
   veal loin, tomato, capers, 178
   zucchini trifolati, tomato, 214
tuna
   raw tuna, bruschetta, 138
turbot
   poached turbot, salsa verde, 131

vanilla
   chocolate, vanilla truffles, 266
   panna cotta, chocolate, 270
   plum, vanilla, bruschetta, 238
veal
   cold roast veal, fresh tomato, 180
   thick veal chop, lemon zest, 175
   veal loin, tomato, capers, 178
   veal shank, butter, white wine, 176
vegetables see also individual vegetables
   cavolo nero, fennel seed, 226
   fava bean, pea, asparagus, 228
   fennel, tomato, 223

fried eggplant, basil, tomato, 206
fried porcini, parsley, garlic, 217
green bean, potato, 220
half-mashed potato, parsley, 222
roast celeriac, squash, fennel, 224
roast eggplant, tomato, 208
roast porcini caps and stems, 216
roast whole pepper, capers, 210
smashed cannellini, olives, 218
zucchini scapece, 212
zucchini trifolati, tomato, 214

walnuts
   apple, orange, walnut, 237
   coffee, walnut, hazelnut
      cake, 264
   radicchio, walnut, Gorgonzola
      salad, 22
wine
   beef tenderloin, red wine,
      horseradish, 182
   broccoli, red wine soup, 122
   bucatini, sardine, salted
      anchovy, 80
   crab, chile, fennel, 142
   ditaloni, mussels, white wine, 86
   poached turbot, salsa verde, 131
   pork shoulder, slow-cooked, 170
   pot-roast guinea fowl, Marsala, 153
   rigatoni, tomato, beef, red
      wine, 74
   roast chicken, Pinot Grigio, 163
   roast chicken, Vermentino, 160
   roast duck, Valpolicella, 158
   roast grouse, Chianti Classico, 146
   roast partridge, Vin Santo, 152
   roast pheasant, Chardonnay, 150
   roast quail,
      Cabernet Sauvignon, 148
   roast wild duck, Nebbiolo, 154
   roast wild duck, Pinot Bianco, 156
   sea bass, potato, tomato, 132
   slow-roast chicken, vermouth, 162
   taglierini, clam, fried zucchini, 84
   twelve-hour beef shank, 184
   veal shank, butter, white wine, 176

zucchini
   mozzarella, raw zucchini,
      prosciutto, 10
   pea, zucchini soup, 114
   spaghetti, squid, zucchini, 82
   tagliatelle, zucchini, mullet, 96
   taglierini, clam, fried zucchini, 84
   zucchini scapece, 212
   zucchini trifolati, tomato, 214

The Authors would like to thank:

David Loftus, Mark Porter, Lesley McOwan, Fiona MacIntyre, Ian Heide, Matthew Armistead, Vashti Armit, Paul Barnes, Stephen Beadle, Sue Birtwistle, Daniel Bohan, Ronnie Bonetti, Daisy Boyd, Jonathan Conroy, Ros Ellis, Helio Fenerich, Susan Fleming, Imogen Fortes, Daisy Garnett, David Gleave, Ossie Gray, Gillian Hegarty, Theo Hill, Lynsey Hird, Jack Lewens, Sofia Manussis, Antonella Nieddu, Stephen Parle, Charles Pullan, Nina Raine, Theo Randall, Alan Rusbridger, Rosie Scott, David Stafford, Joseph Trivelli, Blanche Vaughan, Pirate Vereker, Ed Victor, Lucy Weigall, Joanne Wilkinson, Sian Wyn-Owen, David MacIlwaine, Richard Rogers, The Staff of The River Cafe.

Published in the United States by Clarkson Potter/Publishers, an imprint of
the Crown Publishing Group, a division of Random House, Inc., New York.
www.crownpublishing.com
www.clarksonpotter.com

Clarkson N. Potter is a trademark and Potter and colophon are registered
trademarks of Random House, Inc.

Library of Congress Cataloging-in-Publication Data
is available on request.

ISBN-13: 978-0-307-33835-8
ISBN-10: 0-307-33835-5

Printed in China

Design by Mark Porter

10   9   8   7   6   5   4   3   2   1

First Edition